James Hong™

SAT* Critical Reading
GAME

○ ?
✕ △

James Hong

with Richard Kirby

James Hong **SAT** Critical Reading GAME

TABLE of CONTENTS

A NOTE FROM THE AUTHOR

James Hong's Story

I'm going to be completely honest with you. I got into a lot of trouble because of the techniques I'm about to teach you.

I'm not joking.

In 2009, I was living the life of a rock star. I owned my own test prep academy, cash was rolling in from my classes, and I felt completely invincible because of the incredible test scores my students were achieving.

This all came to an abrupt halt one fateful day…

The reason? I was basically too good. I don't make this claim lightly. South Korea has the most competitive private education market in the world. Teachers who excel in guiding students to great scores receive acclaim, envy and boat loads of money. I was one of these teachers; in fact I was the best SAT Critical Reading teacher in Korea and I still am.

With this fame came extra scrutiny – "how is this guy managing to beat the test??" was the question many people asked. So one day I got a visit from the Korean IRS (tax authorities), the police and the Ministry of Education and the rest, as they say, is history.

But I'm getting ahead of myself here and you definitely didn't buy this book to hear a sob story from some dude you don't even know. You wanna know how I cracked the test, right?

Let's rewind way back a bit. I'd just graduated Cum Laude from Harvard, majoring in Economics. The future looked bright as I headed off to Wall Street. After a couple of years working in finance, I grew tired of the hectic pace and decided to return to Korea to do something completely different.

I'd always loved standardized tests (I even do them at home now for "intellectual enrichment" haha!) so I decided to enter Korea's intense private education market. I looked at the TOEFL, SSAT, SAT, GRE exams you name it! I finally settled on the SAT.

I was ruthless in my goal to crack the test. Part of it was my own ego ("does ETS really think they can make an exam I can't crack?"); another part was my care for the students I worked with.

I spent a full year studying the test in detail. I got hold of as many released real SATs as I could, took the exam on many occasions and broke down the CR section into many small pieces. It was extremely difficult, time consuming work but totally worth it. Based on what I learned, I began churning out students with an incredible ability to beat the test and achieve top scores. These scores were built on the back of hours and hours of my hard work. Many days I would start teaching at 8am and continue till late at night – prepping, testing, teaching – but I loved every grueling minute of it.

Just as things were going really well, reality slapped me in the face. My school's success and popularity attracted more attention, and eventually, the Korean IRS and the Ministry of Education started to take a closer look at my business. Sure enough, they found something they didn't like. You see, in Korea there are very strict price controls you can charge for tuition. I had gone well in excess of these limits and as a result, I had to pay various fines. My business was completely ruined, my health suffered, and I decided to withdraw from teaching.

During my year away, I had a lot of time to reflect about what I'd done and I realized that I was wrong.

This book is part of me giving back.

In this book, you will learn virtually all the strategies I've deployed with so much success (not all because some can only be learned in person). No longer are my strategies only for the elite but I want to share this knowledge with everyone! It represents the culmination of many years of blood, sweat and tears and I'm very proud of it.

I hope this book and the techniques it contains help you as much as it has helped others.

This book is dedicated to the thousands of students I have taught who were actually my teachers and from whom I truly learned how to beat the SAT!

Yours in study,

JH

Richard Kirby's Story

When James first approached me about helping him write a book on the SAT, I was very dubious. The SAT community in Korea is very small and I was well aware of the "challenges" he'd previously faced with the authorities.

In addition, I too had a number of successful years teaching SAT under my belt and believed most of James' success came from slick marketing. In spite of this doubt, I decided to take a chance and work with him because a number of my former students (who I'd taught AP Economics to) had achieved very impressive SAT scores with James.

What I've learned during this book writing process has honestly surprised me. James' approach which initially seems unworkable actually has a solid theoretical background. In addition, during the "beta testing" phase of this book I saw with my own eyes timid, nervous students transform into confident test takers who weren't afraid and welcomed the challenge of the SAT! Their final score results were equally impressive.

The strategies you read about in this book are radical but they work! You owe it to yourself to at least give them a solid try.

I've been involved in all aspects of education since graduating from college and have taught a range of standardized tests, from AP to SAT to the GRE. I have a Masters degree in education from Harvard and get a real kick out of helping students achieve great scores.

I hope you enjoy this book as much as I have enjoyed writing it!

All the best,

RK

PART I INTRODUCTION

Weakness of other SAT CR Material

The major reason I decided to write a book on the SAT Critical Reading section is that there was simply no effective material designed to help students for this part of the SAT.

I found several major problems with existing test prep material:

Shallow insights: I've reviewed at least a hundred SAT related prep books over the years and (with a few minor exceptions) most didn't teach anything profound or fresh. Most of the books seemed to be dedicated to just explaining what the SAT is instead of how you can go about attacking it. What a waste of paper!

This problem is particularly acute when it comes to critical reading. Prep books seem to treat the critical reading section as an unimportant aside while the Big Boys of Math ("wow look at all the diagrams I can put in!") and Writing ("excellent, now I can explain thousands of grammar rules!") dominate.

The sad truth is that prep books spend more time on Math and Writing because they are easier to explain. No one, and I mean no one, has had the guts to totally take on the critical reading section because it is considered "unteachable." The philosophy of most test prep guides seems to be to superficially gloss over the critical reading section and hope students don't demand their money back!

Most of the larger test prep producers also seem to devote hours and hours to (badly) mimicking the SAT. They produce model test after model test that are supposed to replicate the SAT but often fall short. This seeming obsession with imitating the SAT covers up their overall lack of tools for beating the test.

Out of Date: Some of the material was frankly laughable in the way it revealed certain "strategies." For example, Some books (I won't mention any names here) confidently declared that if there was an extreme word (*e.g.* only, always or never) in the answer choice, that answer choic is a guaranteed to be incorrect.

This is completely false and ETS has for years inserted "extreme" words into correct SAT answer choices. Imagine the thousands upon thousands of students that have eliminated correct answer choices based on this poor guidance. It's a disgrace.

Inflexible: Most current test prep materials consider test takers as a basically uniform group. The exact same strategies are given to all students regardless of their fundamental critical reading levels, the time they have to prepare for the exam, what aspect of the critical reading section is giving them difficulty, etc. All students must follow the exact same instructions no matter where they sit on the SAT critical reading spectrum. Ridiculous isn't it?

Imagine going to visit a doctor who gave every single patient he saw the exact same medication regardless of whether they had a broken leg, the flu or cancer. This is exactly what most test prep guides are doing.

Not widely applicable: Another classic shortcoming in these guides is that their strategies seemed designed for only specific conditions. They expect students to fit into their neat boxes. If you don't fit into one of these boxes, then tough luck – you are on your own. This is not scientific and too random for my liking.

This Book's Difference

Flexible and adaptable: There are some hard rules I insist you follow, but not many. If a rule is set, you can be sure it exists for a good reason and its application is wide enough to warrant its necessity. The vast majority of techniques and approaches of this book are more adaptive in nature.

This adaptability fits with my philosophy on how the SAT should be approached. Not with a dogmatic and regimented style but more like a stream making its way toward the sea. As the stream encounters resistance, it fluidly moves around obstructions to avoid the blockage, keeping in mind its singular objective of reaching the sea.

This is my approach – a calm strategic method that puts you high on a hill as you observe and direct the SAT battle below you.

A 'Moneyball' approach: My strategies are not meant to guarantee you will get a 100% of questions correct – that would be a dishonest and unrealistic claim to make. What this book is all about at the end of the day is smart gambling. Have you ever seen the movie *Moneyball*? If you haven't, this is basically what the movie is about:

> Brad Pitt stars as Billy Beane, a one-time baseball prodigy who flamed out in the big leagues and now works as the GM for the Oakland Athletics, a franchise that's about to lose their three best players to free agency. Unfortunately, the team isn't in a financial position to spend as much as big shots like the Yankees and the Red Sox. Beane realizes he needs to radically change how he evaluates what players can bring to the squad. After he meets Peter Brand, an Ivy League economics major working as an executive assistant for scouting on another team, Beane realizes he's found the man who understands how to subvert the system of assessing players that's been in place for nearly a century.

This radical evaluation system was based on the idea that the Oakland A's didn't need to have the best players to excel. What they needed instead was just a *team* working together that would guarantee they reached a certain statistical benchmarks – that's it! This so called Moneyball approach led to impressive victories for the A's as the season progressed. By just playing smart odds, the A's were able to excel.

So it is with my approach to the SAT. I too am taking a scientific approach to the SAT that is meant to increase your *overall* odds and hence your score. Each technique you learn will slightly increase your chances of getting a question right and slightly reduce your chances of getting it wrong. The change will be marginal but it *will* be amazing when added up over the entire critical reading section.

This is the beauty of my system – it works in the background, quietly building up effectiveness as you practice with it. The more you practice with it, the more effective it will become, and the greater your score will increase.

Made for YOU: This book is made for everyone! This was one of my main goals when I decided to write this book – it must have universal usability. The majority of my strategies work for everyone, irrespective of their base SAT Critical Reading levels. Where a strategy works better for a specific type of student I have made a note of this fact. Even if it seems that some advice is directed at students that have a different level of critical reading ability than you, always be sure to read the material because it all helps to lay a solid foundation!

An anticipatory textbook: I know how you think. This is no idle boast. I can almost guarantee I've worked with a student just like you at some time in the past. This varied teaching experience means I often know what mistake a student will make even before he or she makes it. As you work through this book, I am sure there will be a number of "Wow how did he know what I was thinking?" moments. It all comes down to my years and years of teaching experience. This focused advice ensures you are getting the information you want as you need it!

Built on a foundation of experience and science: You know what really gets to me? When I start working with a student who has already learned SAT "strategies" that are at best superficial and at worst plain wrong (*e.g.* avoid "extreme words").

I think teaching the SAT is an incredible responsibility. After all, this is a student's future I am talking about! Badly written SAT material will lead to test day problems which will ultimately result in a score below what the student is capable of. The repercussions of a poor score may mean this student cannot gain admission to a college he or she was completely capable of being accepted to.

There seems to be an idea among those who produce SAT prep material that "something is better than nothing." This is a dangerous philosophy because weak material can do more harm than good!

All of the techniques in this book have been tested and retested and have proven results from among a wide cross section of students. This is how it should be!

Getting your Mind in the Game

As we get into the basics of this, I'd like to tell you a story that illustrates the approach you need to this book.

Y.E. Yang realized he was in deep trouble. A Korean-born professional golfer in his late thirties, he was ranked a dismal 416th in the world. With his age and poor ranking, he realized time was running out for him and he needed to do something fast or face a dismal march into total obscurity.

Yang's solution was radical and risky – he decided to totally reinvent his swing from scratch. For a professional golfer of his age to attempt such a thing was considered complete madness! Yang thought differently. He knew he had everything to gain and nothing to lose.

If his new approach didn't work, so what? He could always return to his old swing. However, if he did succeed and this new swing worked the way he hoped, the sky would be the limit! Yang took a gamble, but not a shot-in-the-dark kind of gamble. He was very scientific about the changes he made to his swing and every change he made was backed up with solid evidence. Sound familiar?

Yang pushed ahead with his new swing and guess what? It totally worked! It worked so well he won the 91st PGA Championship. This victory was the first major championship for a male player born in Asia! Not too bad for a gamble huh?

This is the mindset I want you to have as you approach the techniques and strategies in this book. Put yourself out on a limb, take a gamble and be bold! You have absolutely nothing to lose and everything to gain.

A word of caution before you begin: you must be all in. Half measures don't work with my technique. You cannot choose to follow some strategies but ignore others and students who follow only parts of the strategy will see only the smallest improvement. Why? Because they aren't letting Moneyball completely work its magic, they are disabling parts of the system so it can't work at full power.

What kind of Score Boost to Expect

Moving forward with this mindset, let's talk about the results you will probably see when you use this book.

First off, this book is not a miracle cure that will instantly see you cranking out an 800 in the CR section. These strategies take time and effort to practice and without both of these things, a student will be disappointed with the results.

I believe a consistent 50 point plus increase in *average* score represents a significant improvement in a student's score. What is this based on? In my experience, a student's score varies plus or minus 50 points in tests. So let's say on average you score 600 on the SAT you can expect to score around a 550 on an extremely bad day and around a 650 on an extremely good day. Does this mean your fundamental critical reading skill has changed? Nope. It is exactly the same and no matter how many test you take, it will bounce around within that range.

A fundamental increase in your score occurs when you increase your average score! For example, suppose you read a lot more, memorized vocabulary etc. and managed to lift your average score to 620. Now your worst case scenario is 570 and best is 670. This is a fundamental change!

The reason I stress this is because the majority of prep providers are NOT shifting your critical reading average. They are just throwing strategies that will hopefully increase the chances you score in the higher end of your range (600-650). The problem with this is that they haven't given you a strong base, so you are always susceptible to plunging back down into the lower end of your range (550-600) depending on what variables you encounter on test–day. This is why students get dispirited with prep courses because the latter situation frequently occurs.

Score Improvement Map:

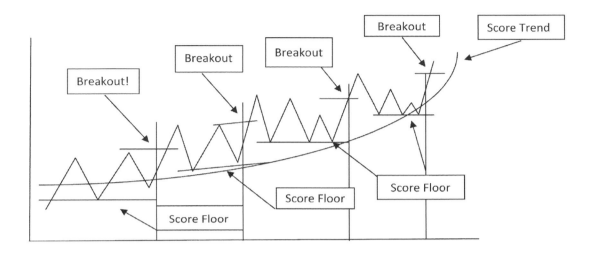

The above graph illustrates the typical progress of a student who uses my system. Initially there is no change in his or her base score and the student's scores on various model tests move within the expected 50 point range. After a certain point, however, the student breaks through the 50 point ceiling and creates a totally new critical reading paradigm for himself. This new paradigm results in a slightly higher average with a higher ceiling and floor

The important thing to notice though is the student will *never* score below this new score floor again. This is because his mind has made a statistically significant improvement in its understanding of the test! This process continues on and on for as long as the student is willing to faithfully practice and apply the system.

This is how this book and the techniques work. I am training your mind to increase its average SAT Critical Reading score so that you have a solid base that can never be eroded no matter how difficult the test is or how poorly you feel on test day!

Why should you even care about all of this? Why not just focus on Math and Writing where score increases are much easier to get?

The reason it is important is the same reason why you take the SAT – to get into a good college. Critical reading is arguably the most important section in SAT because it tests the skills that colleges value the most – the ability to summarize, the ability to draw out from within the text the core essence of what an author is attempting to communicate, the ability to read quickly and effectively under pressure and locate important information that supports a position.

These are all skills that you must have in order to succeed in college. Logically then, the greater the amount of these skills you possess, the more valuable you will appear to prospective colleges. This is why you should and must attempt to conquer the SAT Critical Reading section!

Where You're Headed with This Book

Now I'd like to turn to a basic roadmap of where you'll be going as you learn and begin to master this system.

Stage 1 - A change in mindset and attitude: As you begin working on these techniques, you'll notice your perspective on the SAT changing. As you learn the tricks and traps of the exam, you'll gain confidence because you know the beast, you know how it moves and best of all, you know how to beat it at its own Game!

This change in mindset can have tremendous benefits as you transform from having a myopic view of the test to a commanding vision of the critical reading section. This confidence will translate into you pushing yourself harder and harder to bump up your score. A virtuous cycle will be formed, as the more confidence you have, the harder you will practice and the more your score will grow.

Think of a mouse in a maze searching for a block of cheese. You are the mouse and the correct answer choice is the cheese. If you are one of the lucky few students who have an 800 base SAT Critical Reading level, finding a path to the cheese is relatively straightforward. If you are a student with a lower critical reading level, your route to the cheese will not be as obvious. The key point to remember here is although the route to the cheese is not as obvious, it is still possible to find it!

You must have a 'can do' and 'want to do' attitude as you approach the test because it makes a tremendous difference! Approach the SAT as a Game (which it is) and I will show the rules, tricks, and strategies of the Game, so you can head out and do your best to win. Forget the word 'test' or 'exam' – from now on you only know of the SAT Game!

Simply put, SAT success = your brain (not necessarily your reading power) + your positive attitude + my technique.

You already have the first and since you have bought this book you have gone a long way in achieving the second! The final element will be delivered to you in the coming pages.

All the pieces you need to achieve success in the Game are set – you just have to grab them and create your own destiny.

Stress free, psyched up and ready to go! You should be like this because the goal of the Game is to find the cheese, not to understand everything in the exam.

My technique is focused on this game style approach so if you don't have perfect CR ability – great! The Game is simply more challenging and fun for you. Pity the students with their 800 CR ability because they won't be able to use as many of the techniques as you can to win the Game – how boring!

Stage 2 – Macro Management: At its very core, Macro Management is about effective time management and giving yourself the time to effectively attack questions. In the Chapter on Macro Management, you'll be given very clear timing guidelines to help you make the most of your time in the exam.

Without going into too much detail here, Macro Management gives you the ability to step back from the Game, take a deep breath, and firmly plant your feet before you get into the smaller details.

Stage 3 – Critical Reading: Improving your critical reading skills is a hard road to walk but completely worth the effort. CR is not a solely SAT specific skill but will deliver benefits to you for the rest of your life! In later chapters, you will learn to interpret the building blocks that are used to create a meaningful passage. Starting from the smallest element (words) to the largest (passage), you will learn how to categorize words, analyze relationships and read blocks of text to understand and interpret the author's purpose.

Stage 4 - Micro Management: Micro Management is focused on the small elements that make up each Critical Reading section – the Questions, the Text and the Answer Choices. In Micro Management, we'll be looking at each of these elements in depth and really taking them apart to understand how they work. Finally, I'll give you a range of attacking strategies that will ensure you select the correct Answer Choice as often as possible!

Where Macro Management was aimed at providing a strategic advantage, Micro Management is aimed at providing a tactical advantage. Where time management is the general on the hill calmly giving orders to his troops, Micro Management is the Special Forces soldier on the ground trained in any number of deadly arts to seek out and destroy the enemy.

Stage 5 – Closing: Closing is an entire art of its own. You may have exceptional Macro Management skills and a superb Micro Management technique, but all the time in the world won't help you if you're down to two seemingly correct answer choices and you cannot figure out which to choose. Therefore you must know how to make the most productive and effective use of the precious remaining minutes of the Game. The difference between a Game taker who knows how to close and one who does not can be more than 100 points in the SAT Critical Reading section alone!

Stage 6 – 800?: A lot of you sitting reading this are probably just looking for a modest increase in score. Why limit yourself? I don't make the claim that everyone is going to get an 800 if they follow my strategy, but a significant number of students I work with eventually *do* go on to score an 800 (usually around 20 a year out of a total number of about 500 students).

If you faithfully apply the techniques you learn in this book, you'll be well on your way to becoming part of this elite group!

I'm a dreamer.

I hope many people apply my strategies and go on to achieve perfect scores. I'd love to see my strategies applied so well by millions of students that ETS is ultimately forced to change the SAT!

This book will not yield perfect understanding of my techniques. While I've done my best to pack everything I know into this book, there are certain limits to how much I could convey. To fill in the gaps, I've created my own website (www.JamesHongSAT.com) and will also be opening Test Prep centers in the U.S. and internationally soon! Visit my website and stay tuned!

Finally, here is the list of things you will need before you move onto the next Chapter.

- A copy of *The Official SAT Study Guide*, 2nd Edition published by The College Board (also known as the "Blue Book"). This is a *must have* item and without it this book is useless.
- A timing device – a stopwatch would be best because it is accurate and comes with minimal distractions but any timing device should be sufficient. Don't use a cell phone though because it is too distracting.
- Pencils and an eraser.
- A highlighter.

That's it! Once you have these items ready, you should be all set.

So what are you waiting for?

LET THE GAMES BEGIN!

PART II **MACRO MANAGEMENT**

Chapter Overview

All games have rules and the SAT is no different! One of most ignored and under managed rules of the SAT is *time*.

Macro Management is basically a time management technique that allows you to become a general rather than a lowly foot soldier. By giving you time to strategically plan and *choose* the battles you want to fight, Macro Management delivers confidence and a noticeable bump in your score.

This is going to be a very interactive Chapter where you'll not only be learning the Macro Management techniques but also applying them to tests in the Blue Book. I'm going to start off by giving you a brief intro into what the Critical Reading section is and what it tests. Then I'm going to ask you to take Test 3 in the Blue Book. I'll use this test as a diagnostic tool to determine your base critical reading skill, what types of errors you are making and how you are coping with the time constraints.

After this chapter, you'll know exactly how to macro-manage in the SAT Critical Reading section. I cannot emphasize enough how important it is to be able to macro-manage correctly. Without mastering this technique, it's doubtful you will be able to improve your SAT score.

After learning the details behind Macro Management, you'll apply the technique to Test 1. I pretty much guarantee that you will see an increase in score between Test 3 and Test 1! This is how confident I am about the power of Macro Management.

Are you ready? Then let's do it!

The Anatomy of SAT Critical Reading

What is Critical Reading?

Here's an interesting irony: people love to talk about the SAT Critical Reading section but few actually stop to consider what it is *actually* testing. Weird right?

If you ask the average student what they are being tested on, they will probably reply "it tests to see how well you read."

Wrong!

Being able to read **critically** is very different from being able to read. Instead of just passively absorbing a text, critical reading is a very active process where there is a constant conversation between the reader and what they are reading (the text).

A good analogy for the process of critical reading is a courtroom cross-examination with the reader playing the role of a lawyer and the text being the witness at the stand.

The witness (text) will make a statement which the lawyer (reader) will then consider. The lawyer then will ask follow up questions for clarification and to try and figure out the witness's intention. Without this constant conversation between the reader and the text, the relationship between the two will fall apart and the search for meaning will be difficult.

This, in essence, is what ETS is looking for – how well a reader is able to interrogate a text, find relationships, dig for meaning and bring clarity to often disparate concepts within the reading.

Think you can do that? Great!

A different way to think about the critical reading section is to ask yourself – why do I even need to take the SAT? At the end of the day, this is an exam that is used by colleges to gauge the Critical Reading ability of a variety of students from different backgrounds. One of the most important skills you need to succeed in college is the ability to read a lot of material and then draw out the most important points contained therein (*i.e.* summarize what is important).

The SAT tests your ability to do just that! By setting time limits and requiring students to have both an ability to be able to summarize material and hone in on specific details within a text, ETS is testing skills that are crucial to subsequent college success.

Specifics of the Critical Reading section

The Critical Reading section is divided into Sentence Completion (SentCom) and Passage Based Reading (PBR). There are 19 SentCom questions in the exam and 48 PBR questions. SentCom is vocabulary driven and examines your ability to understand the meanings of a variety of words and the relationship between these words. PBR also contains vocabulary style questions but the majority of the questions in PBR are focused on being able to summarize, interpret, and discriminate between critical information and supporting details.

Diagram of Critical Reading Section:

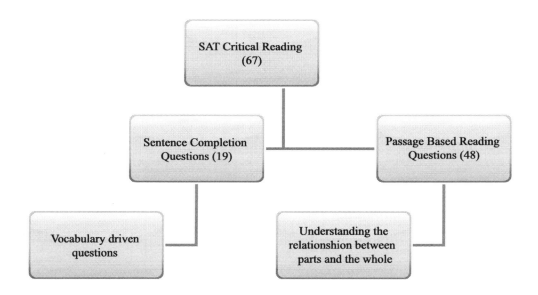

Now it's time for me to stop talking and for you to start doing!

Here's what I want you to do. In the Blue Book (*The Official SAT Study Guide*) please solve all Critical Reading sections of Test 3. Do so as if you were under real SAT conditions (you *must* observe exact SAT time limits).

The reason you'll be taking this test is because I want to get an idea of what your "true" SAT Critical Reading score is (*i.e.* baseline). I'm going to use this baseline score often in later discussions, so please take this test seriously.

You need to meticulously follow these specific guidelines as you take Test 3:

- Don't use any SAT prep tricks or techniques you have previously learned. Attempt the questions in the exact order as they appear in the test – don't jump around at all. Start from question #1 and proceed in sequence to #2, #3…etc.
- When it comes to passages, read the passages first and then answer the questions in sequence. If you have a Double Passage question read both passages first and then answer the questions.
- Walk in a straight line – starting from <u>Page 520 #1</u> and finishing on <u>Page 552 #19</u>.
- Attempt every single question i.e. don't omit any questions.
- At the end of each section, please make a note of the amount of time you spent on that section, and how much time remains. You will need this information later for your score analysis.

After you've completed the test, fill in the SAT Practice Test 3, Scoring Worksheet on Page 559 of the Blue Book.

You As a Test Taker

Understanding your base Critical Reading score

Whatever your ultimate score, if you're an average test taker, you should have a similar percentage of incorrect SentCom and PBR questions. For example, let's say my base SAT Score is 600 – I'd probably get about five SentCom questions out of nineteen incorrect (26%) and about thirteen PBR questions out of forty-eight incorrect (27%).

If the incorrect answer percentages are skewed toward either the SentCom or PBR questions, you need to look at what is taking up the greater percentage of the incorrect answers.

For example, if your base was 600 but you had ten incorrect (50% +) in SentCom and only eight incorrect (17%) in PBR this sends a strong signal. This higher percentage incorrect in SentCom shows where the fundamental critical reading weakness is – vocabulary. It also shows that your ability to see broad themes and structures within texts is stronger relative to your grasp of vocabulary.

In the first scenario, the best way to improve your score would be to focus on boosting your vocabulary (a short term fundamental solution).

This crude but effective improvement method is helpful when you are considering different strategies to improve your critical reading score.

The importance of test taking skills

Up until this point, I've been hammering on about the importance of your critical reading ability, but is this all to the SAT Critical Reading?

In short? No. There is another very important element that is hidden within your Critical Reading score in Test 3 – your test taking ability!

Critical Reading Score Diagram:

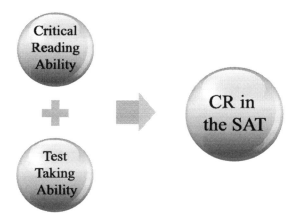

What is 'test taking ability'? Basically these are the skills, methods and techniques that test takers use to solve SAT questions. Here are a few examples of the types of skills that fall under the category of test taking skills:

- Time management and the mental coping mechanisms *i.e.* Part II: Macro Management
- Knowing the types of questions that are on the exam and their nature *i.e.* Part IV: Micro Management - Opening
- Knowing the attributes of correct answer choices and how to find them *i.e.* Part IV: Micro Management - Opening
- Knowing how to decide between two or more confusing answer choices *i.e.* Part V: Micro Management - Closing
- Knowing the attributes of incorrect answer choices and how to avoid them *i.e.* Part V: Micro Management – Closing

These are *not* skills you learn in school, nor do they come from having excellent critical reading ability. Rather, they are skills that must be learned, practiced and perfected if a student is to succeed in the SAT.

This may go against your common sense, and I'm pretty sure you're saying something like, "But this is a *critical reading* exam! You just told me how important it is to be a critical reader!"

You're correct to feel outraged, but my original point is still completely true!

What you need to understand is that these two attributes, critical reading ability and test taking skills, do not operate in isolation but rather work hand in hand!

A Score Increase?

Let's pay a visit to my former student Bill. He was just your average SAT test-taker who was taking the exam because he wanted to go to college.

Bill had never studied for the SAT, and the first time he saw an SAT was on the day he took the exam. Bill believed ETS when they said it's impossible to prepare for the SAT, so he just headed off to his local SAT testing center and took the exam…

What a disaster ☹ – Bill scored a 500 for the Critical Reading section and was completely demoralized because he was actually a pretty good reader. Bill eventually improved but how?

Here's a road map of how he did it:

1) The first thing Bill needed to do was recover to his "true" Critical Reading score (with his critical reading ability, he should've been scoring around 550). To restore his "true" Critical Reading score, he turned to the Macro Management techniques you're learning right now!

2) The second thing he did was supercharge his test taking and critical reading ability for the SAT by applying techniques he learned in Micro Management. These techniques allowed him to explode beyond his base critical reading level by around 100 points.

Score Improvement Trend Table:

Bill's Critical Reading Base	Bill's Test Taking Skill	Bill's First SAT Score	After Macro Management	After Micro Management
				650
550			550	
	Nonexistent	500		

As you can see the ability to test well (Micro and Macro Manage) is what ultimately gives the biggest "bang for your buck" in increasing an SAT score.

You may feel I'm being optimistic but basically here's how it works – I take what you know (and you definitely know something since you can read) and use that to find what you don't know. This back-filling technique is extremely powerful and leads to tremendous score gains in the hands of a dedicated and motivated student.

The test and know yourself

You should never head off to play an important game without knowing all you can about your opponent!

Let's take a look at our opponent ETS, and the exam they've designed.

The SAT Critical Reading section is designed to see if you can *find* specific information, *analyze* it and finally *match* it with a correct answer choice. Sounds straightforward right? It should be but the problem is ETS makes many answer choices look very similar and puts you under time pressure.

In the Game, you will find a variety of questions with different levels of difficulty. ETS uses either a) the difficulty of the main text, *i.e.* the passage, paragraph, etc. or b) the level of difficulty of the answer choices (achieved mainly though making answer choices appear similar and or including higher level vocabulary within them) to set a question's overall level of difficulty.

Two sides to the same SAT coin

The easiest party to blame for difficult question appearing in the SAT is ETS, and this is certainly true. ETS freely acknowledges that there are a variety of questions on the SAT with different difficulty levels (the difficulty level of questions range from 1 to 5).

However, let's be honest – ETS isn't the only party at fault here. The fault also lies with the test taker!

Imagine two test takers, Mr. Complex and Mr. Simple.

When Mr. Complex reaches a level-2 question, for example, he's horrified to find a complex sentence with unknown vocabulary and numerous metaphors and analogies. As he takes in all the details of the question, he becomes overwhelmed by what he's facing. "Oh my, I'll never solve this one!" he might panic.

While Mr. Complex is under siege by everything he sees, calm and composed Mr. Simple ignores all of those same details because he realizes the question is simply looking for a synonym of a simple vocabulary word. Mr. Simple smoothly moves from one question to the next.

Mr. Complex makes a classic SAT mistake – he makes the question harder than it should be. He turns a simple level-2 question into a tricky level-5 question. How? By obsessing over details and not being simple and direct!

The main point I'm making here is that test takers need to know their underlying personalities and testing styles. Test taking personality is an innate quality unrelated to knowledge, skills or expertise – it comes from who you are as a person! What is your personality and testing style?

In my experience, there are two broad groups of test taking personalities. The first category (let's call them 'The Simples') are those who see The Big Picture. They are good at summarizing ideas and don't get bogged down by details. These types of test takers have a real benefit because the SAT rewards this type of approach.

The other category (let's call them 'The Details') are those who construct meaning by looking at small details in the world around them. When reading a passage, The Details target the building blocks that make up the whole idea. While this is a useful skill in the SAT (I use this approach in the Second Round – I'll discuss more about rounds later), it is not as useful as The Simples' approach.

Strength of The Simples: The main strength of The Simples is their ability to simplify and ruthlessly ignore details.

Weakness of The Simples: Later in the test where the ability to see shades of grey between answer choices is needed, this earlier strenghth of The Simples can become a liability.

Strength and Weakness of The Details: The Details are at a disadvantage to The Simples because they struggle with sorting information quickly and efficiently early on in the Game. As the Game proceeds, The Details eye for small differences contained within the answer choices becomes a major asset.

Introducing the Optimal Test Taker

What do I want?

I want you to take positive elements from both The Simples and The Details and create an entirely new Optimal Test Taker (OTT)!

This OTT uses the decisiveness of The Simples to eliminate excessive details and also harnesses the critical eye of The Details to evaluate information.

What is the OTT? Simply put, he's a test-taking machine that has been programmed to do only one thing – attack SAT questions in a methodical manner that leads to the best possible results. What kind of programming does this machine have? I'm sure you know the answer to this: Macro Management.

The OTT is an excellent Macro Manager. He knows exactly what types of questions to attack and when to do it. He doesn't waste time on questions that aren't appropriate for his base critical reading level and excels at simplifying complex concepts and ideas (much more on this to come in this Chapter).

At the right time, the OTT can also change gears and become very analytical in his approach to questions. He's able to see how an argument is constructed and ruthlessly pinpoint information that contradicts what he knows to be the correct answer (much more on this in the Chapter on Micro Management).

A student who is OTT-programmed doesn't care about how difficult a question is or what his underlying testing personality is. This information is irrelevant to him because he runs on an autopilot guided by his OTT programming! I want you to be an OTT specialist.

Refer back to your result from Test 3 and check how much time you had remaining.

I'm going to make a few predictions based on your score for Section 4.

Timing/Question Breakdown Table:

SAT Base	Time you had left on a 25 minute section (+/-)	Questions unable to attempt
750	8	-
700	6	-
650	4	-
600	1 or 0	-
550	Lacking -1 or -2	2+

How can I be so sure that this is the timing/question breakdown? Two reasons: first, I've seen this pattern repeated many, many times over the years I've taught SAT and secondly, it must logically be this way!

A top critical reader would probably misunderstand only a tiny amount of the material in a typical Critical Reading section. For this type of student, finding the answer is a quick straightforward process since he has almost complete understanding.

At lower Critical Reading ability levels, the amount of information that's understood shrinks and the amount that's misunderstood increases. For this student, finding the correct answer is a difficult, time consuming process. This is why there is a relationship between the time a student has remaining and their Critical Reading score.

I love analogies so let's simplify this idea.

Imagine you work as a lumberjack and you've been paid to remove 24 trees in 25 minutes. The trees vary in thickness and so it will take different amounts of effort to chop them down. As an 800 student, you have a powerful chainsaw to complete the job.

You're not the only one who's being paid to cut down 24 trees. Next to you is a fellow lumberjack who is only a 500-level student. This means he will have to tackle the same job with just a small axe!

So, who is going to cut the trees down faster? You, of course, with your supercharged chainsaw!

This is exactly what I've previously described – your tool for attacking the trees is your basic critical reading ability. The higher it is, the faster you'll work and complete the Game!

Is there a way for the lumberjack with the small ax to increase his ability and thus the speed he cuts down the trees? How would this be possible? The answer (I'm sure you're shouting it out) is through Macro Management.

Time Management

Getting your Macro Management on!

In Test 3, I allowed you to work through the test in your own way. Now I want you to change gears and try things my way – I guarantee you'll be happily surprised with the results!

Follow these instructions exactly! ☺ (Note: the instructions are pretty long and detailed and only finish on Page 36, so don't take the test until you've read all the instructions!)

- **Step 1:** Prepare a pencil, eraser and stopwatch and open your Blue Book to Page 390 Test 1. Do not look at any of the questions.

- **Step 2:** Look at the Timing Table on the next page and read the instructions below it…

Timing Table

	Section 2			Section 5			Section 9	
	Allowed Time			Allowed Time			Allowed Time	
	Per Unit	Cumulative		Per Unit	Cumulative		Per Unit	Cumulative
Unit			Unit			Unit		
SentCom (5 Q)	2:30 (__)	2:30 (__)	SentCom (8 Q)	4:00 (__)	4:00 (__)	SentCom (6 Q)	3:00 (__)	3:00 (__)
Short Passage 1 Reading (12 lines)	0:30 (__)	3:00 (__)	Short Passage 1 and 2 Reading (24 lines)	1:00 (__)	5:00 (__)	Long Passage Reading (108 lines)	4:30 (__)	7:30 (__)
Short Passage 1 Questions (2 Q)	1:00 (__)	4:00 (__)	Short Passage 1 and 2 Questions (4 Q)	2:00 (__)	7:00 (__)	Long Passage Questions (13 Q)	6:30 (__)	14:00 (__)
Short Passage 2 Reading (13 lines)	0:30 (__)	4:30 (__)	Long Passage Reading (84 lines)	3:30 (__)	10:30 (__)			
Short Passage 2 Questions (2 Q)	1:00 (__)	5:30 (__)	Long Passage Questions (12 Q)	6:00 (__)	16:30 (__)			
Medium Passage 1 Reading (50 lines)	2:00 (__)	7:30 (__)						
Medium Passage 1 Questions (6 Q)	3:00 (__)	10:30 (__)						
Medium Passage 2 Reading (73 lines)	3:00 (__)	13:30 (__)						
Medium Passage 2 Questions (9 Q)	4:30 (__)	18:00 (__)						
Total Time Taken	18:00 (__)			16:30 (__)			14:00 (__)	
Time Limit	25:00			25:00			20:00	
Bubbling in Time	1:00			1:00			0:45	
Time Remaining	6:00			7:30			5:15	

* Note: Time Remaining = Time Limit – Bubbling in Time – Total Time Taken

James *Hong*™

This Table is your new best friend. You need to follow the timing rules that it specifies, if you want to successfully macro-manage! Let's look at what the Table says:

- *Allowed Time Per Unit:* The maximum amount of time you're allowed to spend on each unit – you can see what a unit consists of by looking at the Units column. For example, the first unit focuses on the first five SentCom questions. For these five questions, you're allowed a maximum of two minutes and thirty seconds (I'll soon explain what you'll be doing during this allowed time).

- *Allowed Time Cumulative:* The amount of time that has past in total. For example, after the first five SentCom questions the cumulative time is 2:30 – since only 2:30 has passed total – while after reading the first Short Passage the cumulative time is 3:00 – the 2:30 you spent on the five SentCom plus the 30 seconds you're allowed for reading the first Short Passage.

- (_____): The time you took to finish the unit.

Sample Time Marking Table:

SentCom (5 Q)	2:30 (2:15)	2:30 (2:15)
Short Passage 1 Reading (12 lines)	0:30 (0:20)	3:00 (2:35)

This student took two minutes and fifteen seconds to complete the first five SentCom questions and then took another twenty seconds to read the first Short Passage. Their cumulative time was two minutes and thirty five seconds. Perfect! Right on the timing money! ☺

The general rules of thumb for successful Macro Management are:

- **All SentCom and PBR questions:** 30 seconds per question (maximum).
- **Reading Passages and Paragraphs:** 30 seconds per reading 12 lines of text (maximum).

Now it's very likely you'll really struggle to meet these timing limits! Don't worry; it's your first time Macro Managing so if you find yourself slipping, don't panic! What you need to do, if your times are off, is mentally change gears and force yourself to be slightly more decisive in attacking questions in a shorter time.

- Step 3: Attempt all questions. What do I mean by *attempt*? An excellent question! Notice I did not say solve but rather attempt – the difference is important! What we're doing here is the "First Round." The objective of the First Round is not to solve questions! Your mission here is purely to sort questions into two different categories – O-questions and X-questions. Below are their definitions:

O-questions: you read the question, read the answer choices and easily find the answer you're looking for (locating the answer should be virtually instantaneous). Now you put a circle around the correct answer and the number of the question. Here is an example of what an O-question looks like:

4. The rhetorical device mainly used by the author in this passage is?
(A) Humor
(B) Sarcasm
(C) Irony
(D) Exaggeration
(E) Analogy

X-questions: you read the question, read the answer choices and cannot find a clear answer (why you can't find the answer is not important), so you omit it for now. And you place an X over the number of this question. Here is an example of what an X-question looks like:

X. The rhetorical device mainly used by the author in this passage is?
(A) Humor
(B) Sarcasm
(C) Irony
(D) Exaggeration
(E) Analogy

Once you have finished a Section, your test pages should be filled with X's or O's.

Something like the following:

(1) A (2) (3) B (4) (5) A (6) C (7) (8) (9) (10) D (11) E …etc.

This is just an example. Your particular combination of O and X-questions will be different. Just make sure you have sorted every question into either the O or X-question category *within* the required time period.

The O-X markings and sorting are all I want you to do during the First Round – nothing more and nothing less. Your singular purpose is to mark each question as either an O or an X question within the time I specified in the Table.

During the entire time you're sorting these questions, keep the following things in your mind:

The "stream" mantra: you're like a stream moving down from a high mountain towards the sea. You have one singular objective – to reach the sea (the last question of the section) in a certain amount of time. To do this, you need to be flexible, moving around obstacles as you encounter them. Always keep moving forward!

Reaction Time: have the same reaction to an unknown SentCom or PBR question as you would have to a completely unknown word in a regular vocabulary test. If you saw the word "opsimath" (an actual word) in a vocab test, would you spend a long time trying to figure it out? Nope! You'd skip it and move on! You should have the same reaction in SentCom or PBR when you reach a question that's very tricky for you – treat it like a completely unknown word in vocabulary test and move on! Students often tend to spend lots of their time trying to "figure out" questions in the SAT when they should have a vocab test-like mentality: "Hey, I don't know this. I'll mark it X and move on!"

Making an X is a mark of strength not weakness: so you've hit an obstacle. There is a question you don't know or you feel you're getting lost like Alice falling down the rabbit hole. What do you do? Smile broadly, mark this as an X-question and move on! Your priority is to stick to the time guidelines and move forward. This might sound repetitive to you, but I might as well say it again because it is that important!!!

Aggressive on X-questions, conservative on O-questions: while sorting questions, don't hesitate in marking them as X-questions. Conversely, be a little more timid when marking as O-questions because you will never come back to these questions later in the Game (unlike the X-questions).

I want you to be totally disciplined with yourself here:

You must stick to the required times outlined in my Table! Force yourself to move on to the next unit if the permissible time on a specific unit expires. Here is the total amount of time you can spend on each Section in the First Round – stick to it!

- **Section 2 - 18 minutes**
- **Section 5 - 16 minutes**
- **Section 9 - 14 minutes**

▪ Step 4: In the Time Remaining (Time Limit minus Total Time Taken), you can return to the X-questions and attempt to solve as many of them as possible. For example, if you'd perfectly macro-managed Section 2, you would've sorted questions for 18 minutes and had about 6 minutes left for attempting to solve as many X-questions as possible (we always assume about one minute for bubbling in on the Answer Sheet). If you hadn't macro-managed successfully and had spent say 20 minutes on sorting, then you'd only have four minutes left for solving the X-questions.

Simple right?

Now that you have your instructions, sharpen your pencil, grab your Blue Book, turn back to the Timing Table, set your stopwatch and let's get going on *macro-managing* Test 1!

I'll wait patiently for you here. ☺

An Analysis of Test 1

Three things are important to you in this Test 1:

- Whether you faithfully stuck to the time limits in the Table and how much time remained after the First Round.
- How many O-questions you marked.
- Among O-questions, how many were ultimately correct and incorrect.

Please count the total number of O and X-questions you had from the First Round and fill in the following Table (I've included an example of a 500-level student for your reference).

A 500-level student's Table:

	Section 2		Section 5		Section 9	
First Round	O	X	O	X	O	X
Total	12	12	12	12	10	9

Your Table:

	Section 2		Section 5		Section 9	
First Round	O	X	O	X	O	X
Total	15	9	12	12	11	8

The number of correct O-questions gives an indication of your true critical reading ability. Why? You've freed yourself from rigid test techniques and are displaying your true reading abilities thanks to Macro Management.

I'm sure at this stage you're curious about what a balanced O-X combination looks like. Great question! Here is a crude guide of the ideal O-X combinations for students with various critical reading ability levels.

Ideal O-X Combination Table:

	Section 2		Section 5		Section 9	
	O	X	O	X	O	X
700-800	18	6	18	6	14	5
600-700	14	10	14	10	11	8
500-600	12	12	12	12	10	9
400-500	9	15	9	15	7	12

Where do these numbers come from? Let's look at a 600-700 level student with excellent Macro Management skills. This type of student should be marking about fourteen questions as O and a further ten as X in Section 2.

Why?

The reason is simple: their basic critical reading ability gives them the "right" to attempt these fourteen questions. ETS is saying "Hey man, I like your awesome 630-reading level so I'm going to give you these 14 questions for free!"

A greedy 630-level student might say "No! I want all 24 free!" to which ETS will reply "Sorry bro, your 630-reading level just gives you the right to try 14 questions for free. You need a higher critical reading level to try more."

A 700-800 level student would have the right to try even more free O-questions in the First Round (18 in fact).

The point I'm making is this: take what is due to you in the First Round! Embrace these free questions, be proud of them – you earned the right to attempt them with your critical reading ability.

But don't be greedy and try grab questions that don't belong to you – don't fight over '*em*, mark '*em* X!

When I was a kid there was this game called "1945." You flew around in this World War II fighter plane and had to shoot down the enemy planes. Of course as you flew around, the enemy was shooting back and eventually the whole screen would be filled with their bullets, lasers, and missiles.

Luckily, the game gave you three bombs which you could drop and destroy everything on the screen! Awesome right? This is what an X-question is – you're flying into enemy territory and the further you go into a question, the more confusing things get. What do you do? Drop your bomb! Make that an X-question and move on. But beware – you only have a limited supply of bombs. Use them wisely!

See how the SAT mimics games! ☺

What happens if you have either too many O or too many X-questions for your level after completing the First Round? Simply put, you have a problem. If you have too many O-questions, you're probably going to end up getting a lot of them incorrect. You're being too aggressive and over-estimating your critical reading ability.

On the other hand, if you have too many X-questions, you'll suffer in the Second Round (*i.e.* the time that remains after the First Round sorting process) because you won't have enough time to cover all of them. To avoid this, you need to be more aggressive. Be confident when you know the answer and don't be afraid to mark it as an O-question.

Let's summarize what we have learned about the First Round.

- The First Round is all about managing your time and sorting questions correctly.
- Strict timing rules need to be followed in the First Round to ensure you move at a good pace
- You're *only* entitled to mark a certain number of O-questions in the First Round based on your critical reading ability.
- If your O-X combination is different from the optimal combination I provided previously, you need to be either more aggressive or more conservative in your marking.

Finally, let's examine the number of First Round O-questions for the 500-level student.

A 500-level Student's O-questions breakdown:

	Section 2 O-questions		Section 5 O-questions		Section 9 O-questions	
Total	12		12		9	
Result	Correct	Incorrect	Correct	Incorrect	Correct	Incorrect
Total	11	1	12	0	8	1

Do the same for your First Round O-questions. Check how many of them are ultimately correct and incorrect (you can check the answers on Page 432).

Your O-questions breakdown:

	Section 2 O-questions		Section 5 O-questions		Section 9 O-questions	
Total	15		12		11	
Result	Correct	Incorrect	Correct	Incorrect	Correct	Incorrect
Total	9	6	12	0	9	2

If I saw a breakdown like what we have for our 500-level student, I'd probably go out and buy him dinner! What makes me so happy?

This student knows two things which are very important for SAT success. First, he knows nearly *exactly* what questions he is "allowed" to attempt with his 500-level reading ability – a correct number of O-questions for his level. Second, when he attempts these questions he mostly gets them right!

If instead I found the student getting many of his O-questions wrong, I'd probably be a bit worried because it would signal that the student is either a) attempting questions that aren't appropriate for his critical reading level or b) he doesn't *truly* understand the characteristics of a correct or incorrect answer choice.

.Both of these weaknesses would point to either poor critical reading or Micro Management skills – something I'll address in detail in later Chapters.

Remember: you can always return to an X-question but never an O-question so when you are sorting, make sure you're not too aggressive with your O-question marking.

As you continue to practice your Macro Management technique, keep an eye on the ratios I discussed previously to see how you're improving.

Turning to the Second Round

Let's return to my imaginary 500-level student and dig further into his results.

A 500-level Student X-questions breakdown:

	Section 2 X-questions		Section 5 X-questions		Section 9 X-questions	
Total	12		12		9	
Result	Correct	Incorrect	Correct	Incorrect	Correct	Incorrect
Total	4	8	5	7	5	4

And you can do the same for your own results.

Your X-question breakdown:

	Section 2 X-questions		Section 5 X-questions		Section 9 X-questions	
Total	9		12		8	
Result	Correct	Incorrect	Correct	Incorrect	Correct	Incorrect
Total	2	7	6	6	3	5

Honestly, whatever your results here, *don't* worry too much about it. While the results certainly do provide some insights into you as a test taker, they're not as important as what we previously covered with Time and O-questions. We will attack these X-questions in detail later in the chapter on Micro Management.

Briefly, the first thing you should notice from the 500 student's Table is his excellent Macro Management skill. He has an appropriate number X-questions for his 500-base critical reading level.

There is also some new info here – the number of X-questions this student subsequently got correct or incorrect.

Is there something "wrong" with the student eventually going on to get eight of his X-questions wrong (Section 2)? *Absolutely not.* This number of incorrect answers is totally appropriate for a student with a 500-level critical reading ability.

Am I saying that this student must just accept that he will always get eight questions wrong among his twelve X-questions? Nope! The techniques you'll learn in Micro Management later on in this book will begin to change this ratio of correct to incorrect X-questions, slowly but surely.

<u>Solution for Macro Management</u>

If you've got a serious imbalance of the O-X combination or really struggled with following the timing guidelines, I'm going to introduce you to three tools that may be able to help you – *The Abandon Ship, Triangle and Backward Method.*

Abandon Ship!

What's the logic behind Abandon Ship? Check out the following Table.

Abandon Ship Table:

	Section 2			Section 5			Section 9		
	Time Remaining	X	Time Deficit	Time Remaining	X	Time Deficit	Time Remaining	X	Time Deficit
600	6	9	-	7:30	9	-	5	7	-
500	6	12	-	7:30	12	-	5	9	-
400	6	15	+/-2 minutes	7:30	15	+/-2 minute	5	12	+/-2 minutes

* Note: the assumption behind the deficit column is that it takes approximately 30 seconds to solve a question.

What do you notice? Students with lower scores will not have enough time to attempt all questions in the Second Round. For example, a 400-level student will be short by approximately 2 minutes.

The solution? Abandon ship! Very low level students must completely ignore a certain number of X-questions and focus their precious time on the questions they can attempt. Here are the specifics.

Base Reading v. Questions to Abandon Table:

Base critical reading	Approx number of questions to abandon per section
500+	None
High 400's	3
Low 400's	3-4
High 300's	4
Low 300's	4-5

As you can see, if you are a 500+ level student, you must attempt to solve every question.

Rule of thumb for everyone: the number of minutes you have left after the First Round multiplied by two is the maximum number of questions you can cover in the Second Round. So, if you have five minutes left and twelve X-questions, you can cover about ten X-questions and you completely abandon two.

Side Note: To Omit or Not to Omit? Never omit! Take a look at the following Table to see you should never omit:

Omission Table:

Questions Correct	Questions Incorrect	Theoretical Penalty	Actual Penalty
67	-	-	-
66	1	0.25	0
65	2	0.5	0
64	3	0.75	1
63	4	1	1
62	5	1.25	1
61	6	1.5	1
60	7	1.75	2
59	8	2.0	2
58	9	2.25	2
57	10	2.5	2

If you get 1 or 2 questions wrong, your actual score penalty will be exactly the same (i.e. 0). If you get between 3 and 6 questions wrong your score penalty will be exactly the same (i.e. 1). If you get between 7 and 10 questions wrong your penalty will be…exactly the same (i.e. 2)! What this shows is that after you move into a new "penalty bracket" (e.g. from 3-6 incorrect to 7-10 incorrect), you need to get three more questions wrong before you'll be penalized again. Thus it's very much in your interests to never omit a question and take that chance that you could be correct! On the other hand, if you get even one of these guesses correct, you'll instantly lift your raw-score by one full point!

The Triangle

The Triangle is only allowed to be used in exceptional (and I mean exceptional) cases.

You use a Δ- question when you have too many X-questions after the First Round (way beyond the number you should have for your critical reading level). For example, a 500-level student has 18 X-questions but only 6 O-questions.

A triangle question, unlike an O-question ("I'm immediately sure I know the answer to this question") or an X-question ("I don't know the answer to this question"), falls in the grey area between the two.

word of warning: this marking method should *only* be used when a student has way too many X-questions and only a few O-questions (compared to the optimal ratio of O-X questions for his or her critical reading level).

Why?

Every question in the First Round *should* be sorted into the O-X categories. Marking a Δ-question is a poor substitute for a clear black-and-white XO combination.

To be able to mark a question as Δ-questions you must either:

a) know the answer but find two answer choices that seem to fit (one answer choice should seem like a slightly better fit) or;

b) *not* know the answer but can eliminate three obviously incorrect answer choices, leaving you with two answer choices (one answer choice should seem like a slightly better fit).

Only then can you mark this as a Δ-question.

Δ-questions should help you relax by decreasing the number of X-questions to a manageable number.

An example of a Δ-Question:

4. The rhetorical device mainly used by the author in this passage is?
(A) Humor
(B) Sarcasm
(C) Irony
(D) Exaggeration
(E) Analogy

The above example shows that I feel (A) and (C) *could* be correct with (A) *probably* more correct.

In the Second Round, I want you to attack X-questions first and the Δ-questions last, because if you're running out of time, you can always mark the answer sheet with the Δ-question answer choice you identified. However, if you're so pressed for time after the First Round, start working on the Δ-questions first because they will require the least amount of time to solve (since you have already narrowed the number of possible Answer Choices) and you will have a greater chance of getting these questions correct.

The Triangle as a measurement tool

Another strength of Δ-questions is that they're a good measuring tool.

After taking more practice tests, if you find many of your Δ-questions are ultimately correct, this shows you that you're being too timid and need to be more confident in following your instincts. Mark more Δ-questions as O-questions!

A very different signal is being sent if you find many of your Δ-questions are ultimately incorrect. Here there is an understanding problem that could be connected to any part of the Game (the questions? the text? the answer choices?). Unfortunately, there is no quick fix solution here but I'll give lessons on each of these parts of the Game as the book progresses.

As you continue practicing, you should reduce the number of Δ-questions till you only have XO-questions. Remember, XO-questions are superior to Δ-questions.

'Backward' versus 'Forward' method

Is each Critical Reading section built in exactly the same way? Nope.

There are different combinations of questions/passages in the Game but by far the most common are:

> **5/4/6/9 – As in Section 2:** five SentCom questions, four Short Passage questions, six Mid-size Passage questions, and nine Mid-size Passage questions.

> **8/4/12 – As in Section 5:** eight SentCom questions, four Short Passage questions, and twelve Long Passage questions

> **6/13 – As in Section 9:** six SentCom questions, and thirteen Long Passage questions.

The difference in section structures is important because of time! Basically the more reading and questions there are in a section, the more time pressure you'll be under.

Which section style do you think will give you the biggest time challenge?

Bingo! The 5/4/6/9 section with its four different tasks and around 140 lines of reading will be the biggest challenge (next most challenging is the 6/13 Section). Keep a close eye on your timing in this section.

If I'm working with students who are struggling to meet their timing deadlines, I often recommend they use 'the backward method' for attacking the 5/4/6/9 section, because this method saves an impressive amount of time.

What exactly is the 'backward method'?

The 'backward method' is basically:

1) You only read the italicized blurb at the top of the passage, ignore the passage and then immediately move to the questions.
2) Skip any General Questions you encounter – General Questions do not have a line reference.
3) Attempt to solve *only* Detail Questions with a line reference by reading the part of the passage the question refers to.
4) Finally, try and solve the General Questions, using the general theme you could probably come up with after you've solved the Detail Questions.

The easiest way to understand the 'backward method' is to compare it to the 'forward method.' The 'forward method' is the way you've solved reading comprehension questions your whole life – you read the text and then answer the question. Simple right?

The 'backward method' is based on a value judgment that time left in the Second Round is more important than perfectly understanding passages! The greater your reading and comprehension skills, the more you can use the 'forward method.'

Here's a Table to guide you.

Forward/Backward Table:

	5/4/6/9	8/4/12	6/13
700+	Forward	Forward	Forward
600-690	Backward	Forward	Forward
500-590	Backward	Forward	Backward
300-490	Backward	Backward	Backward

* Note: Use the backward method only for a MId and Long Passage. Always use the forward method for a Short Passage.

If you're a student with a limited time left till the SAT (less than 2–3 months) follow this Table. If you've got a lot of time for preparation, use the forward method as long as you're sticking to the timing rules because forward is ultimately superior to backward. Forward is the technique of choice for SAT and it's the method you'll use most throughout your life (especially in college) so you might as well perfect it now!

A Final Word

You're a racing car entering the SAT race with a certain engine size.

The size of your engine depends on your test taking ability and critical reading level. The greater your engine size, the greater power you have for delivering an amazing performance on race day!

Macro Management is your engine in the SAT. Without a powerful engine, it doesn't matter if you install fancy new tires or change your brand of fuel– a small engine makes any superficial changes irrelevant! This is how critical solid Macro Management skills are.

Here's what I want you to be like: a general perched on a hill surveying the battlefield. You observe the battle happening at your leisure and calmly give commands to your troops. You have this composure, broad perspective, and time because you have excellent Macro Management skills!

Compare this to a pitiful foot soldier stuck in his foxhole with explosions all around him and no idea what is going on. This is what a student with poor Macro Management feels like – they have no control, they have no perspective, they have no time!

Due to space constraints in the book, I wasn't able to include things like:

- Specific Tips on improving the marking reaction time.
- Timing Tables for each of the Tests in the Blue Book.
- How to Effectively use the Triangle,
- More detailed lessons for the Forward and Backward method for optimal testing results.
- The particular number of questions you should mark O or X, depending on your base critical reading level.

For information on the above, please visit our website or one of our Test Prep locations.

PART III

CRITICAL READING

Chapter Overview

Are you struggling with reading critically? Are you a good critical reader but still finding it difficult to make the change to SAT-style critical reading?

No problem! This is the chapter for you!

This chapter is basically about learning how to read words, word pairs, sentences, paragraphs and passages to extract objective meaning. You'll also be learning the difference between objective and subjective reading and why it's so important for SAT success.

Are you ready? Great!

Let's dive into critical reading with a visit to my friendly critical reading doctor!

The Table Method

A visit to the eye (reading) doctor

Ever had your eyes tested? What happened?

You stood at one end of a room, put your hand over an eye and gazed at a distant chart filled with letters. Starting at the top of the chart the doctor would ask you to tell him what letter he was pointing at. Gradually, he'd move down the chart and as he did, the letters would get smaller and smaller.

Eventually, you wouldn't be able to see what letter the doctor was pointing at. The letters would be hazy and you'd have to really squint to figure them out.

The better your eye-sight, the more details you could see and the further down the chart you could read.

After the test the doc would present you with a test result that ranged from a perfect 20 to a below average 5

So it is with reading! When you read, you also have either an excellent ability to understand everything you read or a more basic ability to only figure out a few details from what you've just read.

Eye test measurement and reading

Let's look at a sentence together:

The **river** violently **flooded** after a heavy storm.

Forget reading – which word is the easiest to see? The word "river" right? This word is the biggest in the sentence. What about next? Bingo! "Flooded" is the next biggest word in this sentence. If you had great eyesight, you could probably also make out the rest of the words but they would be more of a challenge.

The sentence normally:

The river violently flooded after a heavy storm.

Now imagine someone in a panic ran up to you and excitedly shouted this sentence in your face before running off again. What bit of information would your brain latch onto first?

River

What piece of information would your brain latch onto next?

Flooding

Putting these two together, you'd probably react with an "Oh #$%! This is bad!"

This is exactly how your brain processes information as you read.

Sentence Table:

	"The river violently flooded after a heavy storm"
5	River
10	Negative (−)
15	Flooded
20	violently, after a storm

Let's explore this little Table in a bit more detail:

The topic (also known as the 5) – the subject of the sentence and the easiest piece of info to find (very prominent), i.e. river.

The evaluation (also known as the 10) – go on instinct with this one – does the information you are reading leave you with a positive (+), negative (–) or neutral feeling when you read it? This is subjective but, as you'll soon find out, words, sentences and paragraphs all come with their own "feeling" attached. Your "Oh #$%!" clearly shows that this particular sentence comes with a negative feeling attached hence the (–) in the 10 row.

The theme (also known as the 15) – this provides more information about the topic, e.g. flooding. It's a kind of loose summary of whatever you're examining. I'll talk more about themes later.

The details (also known as the 20) – Any finer details that surround the topic and theme are details.

The previous Table is your new best buddy and gaming partner! You'll take him along with you as you tackle various SAT questions. Don't worry if you're still unsure on how to apply what I call the Table Method – you'll soon have lots of practice!

Keepin' it real with the Table Method and Vocab

I'm going to throw you in the deep end because I know you're ready!

My previous example used the Table to dissect a sentence. The same is possible for vocabulary? Oh yes! Check out these words.

Word Table:

	Criminal (Noun)	Diligent (Adjective)	Besiege (Verb)
5	Person	Description	Action
10	–	+	–
15	Immoral	Hardworking	Attacking and harassing
20	* See next page	e.g. working hard	e.g. surrounding during warfare

Let's start with the word "criminal." Fundamentally, what are criminals? They're people – there are no such things as criminal objects or places! This is the topic (5) – the easiest info to 'find' from this word.

Does the idea of a criminal relaxing outside your house leave you with a good or bad feeling? I'm going to guess you wouldn't be happy about this, so the evaluation of this word is bad or negative.

Remember, the theme (15) gives you more info about the topic. What kind of person is a criminal? Simply put – someone who acts immorally. Nice, now you have found the theme!

The detail (20) of a word includes all possible uses and definitions of the word "criminal." For example, you could also use the word criminal to describe extremely high prices at a bar as in "These beer prices are criminal!" But don't worry too much about the 20 at this stage.

Congrats! You've just dissected your first word – the other two words in the Table follow the exact same logic.

Now I'd like to take a break while you create a Table for the following words: "blockade," "encircle," and "hound" (all verbs). Please do this before moving on to the next step.

Word Table:

	Blockade	Encircle	Hound
5 (topic)	Action	Action	Action
10 (+/–/N)	N	+	+
15 (theme)	Seal	circle around	harass
20 (detail)	harbor blockade	encircled town	hound for $$

Here is my Table for these words.

Word Table:

	Blockade	Encircle	Hound
5	Action	Action	Action
10	—	—	—
15	Attacking and harassing	Attacking and harassing	Attacking and harassing
20	e.g. blocking	e.g. circling	e.g. chasing

It's likely many of you thought that "blocking," "circling," and "chasing" were themes (15) here - but that's incorrect. These words are too specific and are closer to definitions and therefore details (20).

What are you noticing in this Table? Right! The 5, 10 and 15 of these words are identical. This is no coincidence since they're considered close synonyms for the purposes of the SAT ("besiege" is also considered a close synonym for these words).

"So what" I bet you're saying.

As you'll learn in more detail later, the SAT is basically about matching – word to word, sentence to sentence, theme to theme etc. Your new Table Method gaming buddy is an awesome simplifying tool to help you avoid clutter and match appropriate concepts.

This is not the only benefit of the Table Method - the theme (15) in the Table is a flexible tool for learning and linking vocab! The most inefficient method of matching words is to learn literal meanings *i.e.* you open the dictionary, find a word, write down all possible definitions and then commit them to memory. Ouch!

Themes, on the other hand, give you the ability to "see" meaning hidden in words and eventually make connections. The above words all have a similar theme of "attacking and harassing." It's only when you zoom in to the highest level of magnification (20) that the marginal differences between the words appear.

The good news: for the purposes of the SAT, a word's theme is often sufficient for finding the correct answer when it comes to vocabulary specific questions.

Theme Matching –

Themes, themes and more themes

Because theme matching is such an important concepts, I'm going to look at it from a variety of angles. Let's start by looking at two words, "calculate" and "planning."

If I ran up to you in the street and asked, "What is the definition of the word calculate?" your mind would probably instantly think of a calculator and math class so you'd probably reply, "it means to find an answer, like in math."

"Good work," I'd say followed by, "hey bro, is there any connection between calculating and planning?"

"Nah," you'd probably declare.

There was an SAT question exactly like this where "calculation" appeared in the text and "planning" was an answer choice that it needed to be matched with. If you couldn't find that match, you would've got the question wrong and lost a point.

Let's rewind back to where the problem started. It all started with the rigid definition you decided to give to "calculate."

Instead of considering themes, you immediately went with an inflexible definition precluded the connection to another related word, in this case, "planning."

"Calculate" has another meaning that is *very* similar to "planning" and it is *this* version of "calculate" that is relevant. Here it is:

> Determine by reasoning, experience, or common sense; reckon or judge: "I calculated that she had been on vacation"

Compare this to your probable initial definition:

Determine (the amount or number of something) mathematically.

What is a way to get around these multiple definitions? *Theme matching*! Let's Table these two words.

Word Table:

	Calculate	Planning
5	Action	Action
10	N	N
15	Mental process	Mental process
20	e.g. weighing up different variables to find an answer.	e.g. arranging a method beforehand

The theme of both these words is "mental process." Even if you didn't know the second definition of calculating, by simplifying and summarizing its theme you'd be able see the link with planning.

This theme searching and matching process might seem a bit tricky now, but I promise with practice you'll be experts (especially after you've reviewed Test 1)!

Time for me to relax again and you to get your theme searching on! Please complete the following Table before moving on. There is no link between the words; I just want you to see a bit more theme searching in action.

Word Table:

	Mercenary (Noun)	Charge (Verb)	Crystallize (Verb)	Arrest (Verb)
5	Person	Action	Action	Action
10	−	+	+	−
15	Soldier	forward	to harden	capture, stop
20	hired soldier	moving forward rapidly	turn to crystal	arrest criminal

Here's the Table I came up with.

Word Table:

	Mercenary (Noun)	Charge (Verb)	Crystallize (Verb)	Arrest (Verb)
5	Person	Action	Action	Action
10	–	+	+	–
15	Materialistic	Forward	Fixed, solid	Stop, limit
20	e.g. a hired soldier	e.g. to move rapidly forward in battle	e.g. to turn to crystal	e.g. to capture a criminal

Can you see the themes emerging from each word? The themes are neither rigid definitions nor superficial meanings. They are instead an attempt to draw the *essence* out of a word. If you're having difficulties with this concept, think of a coffee maker.

Do you just put coffee beans straight into your cup? Nope. Why not? Because if you did, you'd have super weak coffee and a bunch of beans floating around! So what's the solution? You grind the coffee beans, put them in a strainer and then slowly drip hot water over them in order to *draw out the coffee's essence*.

Rigid definitions of words are the coffee beans – useful to have but you'll need a lot of them to make one cup of coffee and find a match. The pure coffee essence is the theme of the word – exactly what you need to make your coffee and to make vocabulary matches.

If the words you chose for the themes are close synonyms or you feel they're thematically similar to my words, you've hit the target! If not, maybe you're taking a too literal, dictionary style approach to the words.

Moving out of the literal zone

Why is it dangerous to live in Dictionary Definition Land (DDL)? To show you the danger, let's explore DDL, using the word "arrest" as a guide.

Here's a nice SAT prompt sentence to start us on the journey:

> The priests <u>arrested</u> the number of people moving to cities by providing allowances to farmers.

If you used the most obvious meaning of the word "arrested," this sentence would seem very strange. You might be asking yourself, "Why would people be arrested by priests for moving to the cities and why are allowances mentioned??"

All very good questions! You're starting to see the dangers of DDL. So how are you going to figure out what arrested means in this sentence?

Right! You're going to dig into the theme behind "arrested" to work it out.

What images jump into your head when you hear the word "arrested"? Police, handcuffs, prison etc. All these images have one theme in common – limits on movement. Now you're getting somewhere.

The meaning of the sentence is becoming clearer. The priests were giving money to people to stop them from moving to the cities. So "arrest" in this context means to stop or limit. Excellent!

You're starting to get it right? ☺

Let's try more. Please fill in the Table below.

<u>Word Table:</u>

	Perfect	Attract	Appoint
5	Description	Action	Action
10	+	+	N,
15	Complete	bring to getwr	placing
20	flawless	good looking	appointed to a position

Roots and the search for meaning

Themes work in parallel with a friend – word roots!

Word Table:

	Perfect	Attract	Appoint
5	Description	Action	Action
10	+	+	N
15	Completely made	Bring closer	Placing
20	e.g. the best	e.g. physically appealing	e.g. to place in a certain position.

In some cases, you may be faced with a word that just doesn't seem to fit in a sentence (if you follow the definition in your head). Your first instinct should be to try and dig into the theme behind the word and expand the meaning. However, this method is not foolproof because in some cases, you won't even know the theme (*e.g.* arrest has a theme of stopping). So what can you do now?

You turn to word roots. Let's try it out!

If you don't know the theme of "attract," you could start your theme search by looking at the root "tract" which is to pull towards (think of a tractor pulling a plough). Other related root words include retract and detract (which has the opposite meaning – to take away from something). So the theme I could draw from this root would be to "bring closer." For example, "the lymph nodes 'attract' body infections."

Roots can also guide in finding the theme for "perfect" – "per" (*pervade, per*spective, *per*emptory) as in being thorough and "fect" (manufacture or factory) as in being able to make. So "perfect" becomes "thoroughly made." Nice! For example, "the politician wants to be politically correct so he tends to describe minorities as perfect." In this case "perfect" doesn't theme match with amazing or great, but rather its theme is without flaw (the synonym match would be closer to "innocent" or "virtuous").

Side Note: Exact spelling isn't that important when you're doing root analysis, just as long as the words seem to sound similar e.g. "fect" versus "fact." This of course makes sense since a root has derivatives which don't always have the exact same spelling.

y our root method on "appoint":

> The architect had a clear vision for how the office would be <u>appointed</u> with computer terminals, modern office chairs and sleek, chrome table.

The strict dictionary definition of "appointed" in this context is "furnished."

"Appoint" has a distant root cousin in the word "point" (as in 'I point at you') or a "point" ('a point on a map'). In both cases you're designating or specifying something. So using this broad root theme of "designation," you could imagine the architect pointing out and *designating* what things would be in the office *i.e.* how the office would be furnished!

Remember our prior word of "arrested." We can approach this word in the same way. If we look at the word "arrest" etymologically, it has the root of "rest" which means "pause." Think of the sentence "Have a rest!" So now you have two approaches you can use to dig for meaning in a word.

Cool huh? A little bit of lateral thinking can go a long way in the SAT Game!

Taking your theme weapon to the SAT

The real question on your mind at the moment is probably – "this theme stuff is kind of interesting but will it work in the SAT?"

The proof is in the pudding so let's try it out! In your Blue Book, please look at <u>Page 523 #17</u>. The correct answer is (A) and the key word in the answer choice is "suggestion."

Let's bring our Table buddy in for a bit of help.

<u>Word Table:</u>

	Suggestion
5	Action
10	N
15	Influence
20	e.g. to provide ideas on a complicated matter

If you re-word this sentence, using the commonly understood meaning of "suggestion," you'd come up with something like "the power of giving people advice."

Hmm. There seems like no connection between the text and (A) so how can this be correct?

Time to turn to themes for some help! What happens when someone gives you a suggestion? If your basketball coach gives you a suggestion on how to improve your jump shot or your dribbling, you will consider his suggestion and maybe incorporate the techniques he recommends. Even if you don't take his advice, his suggestions have at least given you something to consider. In other words, the basketball coach has influenced your game, or at least, the way you think about the game. Thus, "influencing" is a theme behind "suggestion."

The many situations highlighted in the text (lines 38-44) are all examples of how some people influence others to yawn. Bingo! Now you can see why there is a match! Theme matching has saved the day once again.

The Context

Leveling up to sentences

Up until this point, we've only considered individual words and their themes. Now we're going to look at how context (*i.e.* various words coming together) can also be useful when we're searching for meaning.

To do this, we're going to look at the following sentences and specifically the word "break":

(A) Dawn broke slowly over the sleepy countryside

(B) John broke the record in the Winter Olympics

(C) The cowboy broke in the wild horse

(D) The son broke down at his mother's funeral

(E) My antique vase dropped and broke last night

The other words in the sentences are easy but "broke" is a bit tricky. So what do you do? You first Table it.

Word Table:

	Break
5	Action
10	+/–/N
15	Change, separate
20	e.g. the act of unmaking something that is complete.

The theme I decided on was "change" because whenever something is broken, it is fundamentally changed. Think of what happens when you drop a glass of water on the floor; the glass fundamentally changes shape – into a bunch of little pieces!

The challenge in the above sentences is that the theme of "change" can only go so far in helping you find out the meaning of the word "break." You have to turn to contextual clues to get you to the true meaning!

To do this, we're going to use our Table and dissect each of the sentences into their basic elements. Here's how they look after being cut up:

Sentence Table:

	(A)	(B)	(C)	(D)	(E)
5	Dawn	John, record	Cowboy, Horse	Son	Vase
10	N	+	N	–	–
15	Change	Change	Change	Change	Change
20	"slowly over the sleepy countryside"	"in the Winter Olympics"	"wild"	"down at his mother's funeral"	"antique", "dropped"

Where are you getting the 5, 10 and 15 from? The topic (5) is both the subject and object of the sentence. This gives you the *limits* within which the theme must be found. So for example, if you have a sentence like "The puppy _____ me," the scope of possible themes is limited to those that a puppy could do to a person – bit, licked, scratched etc. The puppy cannot however talk, debate or drop-kick you! How do you know this? Because you've set the limits with your topic (5)!

The evaluation (10) is a subjective feeling of whether the sentence conveys a positive, negative or neutral feeling. The theme (15) is the verb (remember to dig into the theme of the verb) of the sentence. Finally, the details (20) are the modifiers within the sentence, for example, adjectives, adverbs, subordinating clauses etc.

Let's look at sentence (E) as an example. The subject of this sentence is a "vase" (5) and the fact that it was broken (15) when it was dropped (20) which is a bad thing (10).

With this as a model, let's return now to the previous sentences and the Table.

The topic (5) and evaluation (10) of each sentence in the Table is different. What is the same is of course the theme (since break is the key to unlocking the sentences meaning). Even though the words within the sentences are very different, the themes are all the same!

"Great table," I bet you're thinking, "but how does it begin to help you find out what 'break' means in each of those sentence?"

The answer is staring you right in the face! ☺

The dance between the topic, theme, evaluation and details is your guide to helping you figure out what the word "break" means in each of those sentences, and hence what the whole sentence means!

Let's look at sentence (E) for example. In this sentence, we've figured out that "break" in this sentence is related to a theme of change (15) in a vase (5). We've also evaluated this negatively (10). The detail (20) of "dropped" provides critical contextual clues.

What would've happened to a vase to change it in a negative way after being dropped? It could've smashed or shattered right? Right! There you have it – this is how you can use a theme of a word and its given context to find out the meaning of the word and hence entire sentence.

Using the technique we just discussed try figure out how "break" is used in (A), (B), (C) and (D). While you're working through these four examples, imagine you're tackling a real SAT question. For example assume the question was something like "In the context of the following sentence, "broke" most nearly means?"

Below are my suggestions for their meanings:

(A) starts/begins (B) overcame/beat (C) tamed/trained (D) cried/sobbed (E) crashed/shattered

This simple but powerful one-two punch of using a theme of a word and its given context can go a long way in helping you find out the meanings of seemingly known or unknown words.

Let's bring in a sample SAT question to show the strength of this one-two punch:

In the context of line 27 the word "*broken*" most nearly means? (Let's assume line 27 says "John was completely crushed at his mother's funeral and looked like a *broken* man.")

(A) smashed   (B) deleted   (C) distorted   (D) started   (E) emotionally crippled

I've already done a Table for "*broken*" so I don't need to do it again here. What I do need is a context Table for the sentence.

Sentence Table:

	John was completely crushed at his mother's funeral and looked like a broken man
5	John
10	–
15	Change
20	"crushed", "funeral"

I've made this question a little trickier because all answer choices have a theme of change. This means a theme match alone can't save you. Let's use my contextual technique then.

My evaluation (10) of the sentence was negative. This would seem to eliminate (D) because "started" has a neutral evaluation. This leaves (A) "smashed," (B) "deleted," (C) "distorted," and (E) "emotionally crippled."

What's the topic of the sentence? – John. Now think carefully – could John be "smashed," "deleted," or "distorted" at a funeral? Definitely not – that sounds absurd.

Could John be "emotionally crippled" at a funeral? Yes! Does this an emotionally crippled John imply a change? Yes (he was emotionally healthy before but now he is not)! Bingo! (E) is the answer.

Are you starting to feel the power of your new gaming buddy? The Table Method in the right hands can solve even the most difficult question and sentences!

Take a breather and meditate on what you've learned so far about words:

- Words can have multiple dictionary definitions but becoming a smart SAT Gamer rests not in memorizing every single definition in the dictionary but in finding themes!
- While themes are powerful tools for unlocking meaning, they need help from the context to create true meaning!

You've done well so far and now it's time to climb further up the critical reading ladder!

Searching for meaning within a paragraph and passage

Now we're going to invite another concept to our critical reading party – multiple sentences!

Let's kick-off with an example:

David Robbins, a trailblazer in education policy, embodied the humanness of the academic. The problem of high dropout rates in inner-city schools intrigued and puzzled Robbins, a college professor with some training in development psychology and the humanities.

Q: In context, the word "*humanness*" most closely means?

(A) an emotional connection with people

(B) wanting to be the first to achieve something

(C) studying themes relating to education

(D) curiosity

(E) a college level education

How could you attack this question? You could start by digging into the word "*humanness*" but you wouldn't have much luck. Why? Because the question is asking you consider the word *in the context of the passage.* This means you can't simply look at the word alone or just the sentence it's in – you need to look at the entire paragraph.

Don't worry – this actually makes things a lot easier because you've got more info to work with.

So let's do this! Now that you've been trained to look deeper into words (themes, context etc.) you'll probably realize "humanness" relates to being the qualities of being human.

But this is very vague and only has the potential to eliminate choices (C) and (E) since they don't have a strong connection to "being human." We're left with (A), (B) and (D).

This brings us to a fundamental point when it comes to critical reading – *you must always be curious when you read.*

At the end of the first sentence, you should immediately wonder, "Hmm… why was the Professor considered a good example of a *humanness* of academics?" This sentence is what I call a "half-known" sentence because it begs us to find out more information about what was said.

Imagine this: a friend walked up to you and said, "you know, Steve is fantastic!!" and then walks away. How do you feel? You feel like calling him back and asking him for more info right? "Why exactly is Steve fantastic?" you're probably thinking. If you said this to your friend, he might say, "Ah sorry, he's so fantastic because he got a 2400 in the SAT." Your "half-known" is now completely known because you have total information about Steve.

It's the same in writing. You don't just make a statement and leave it hanging – you must provide support! Where is this author's support for making the claim of "humanness"? It's in the second sentence – "intrigued and puzzled" (synonymous with being *curious*) a characteristic all humans share!

You have a nice one-two punch here with the claim (humanness) BAM! followed up by the support (intrigued and puzzled) BAM!

So the answer is (D).

A sentence where we can get a basic idea of what is being said but aren't 100% sure of the meaning is known as a "half-known" sentence. You'll learn more about these "half-known" sentences later.

Structural Understanding

Putting it all together

Let's up the stakes and put everything we've learned into practice. Grab your Blue Book and turn to Page 57 and let's take apart a Short Paragraph using all the techniques we've explored!

First, I want you to read the upper Passage and then write a one sentence summary of what you read (you can do this below).

_____

Okay! What did you notice about the opening sentence of the first Paragraph? It's a "half-known" sentence – while the words in the sentence are easy to understand, the word combination "peculiar curse" is a bit strange.

As critical readers, this should immediately make you curious – "What does art forgery have to do with a curse?" and "Why is art forgery not just a curse but a peculiar curse?"

Let's create a Table for these words to get a bit more insight.

Words Table:

	Curse	Peculiar
5	Noun	Adjective
10	–	N /+
15	Destined to fail	Uniqueness
20	e.g. used in religion to damn someone	e.g. a quirky personality, a different style of artwork

What do you notice here?

"Curse" has a negative evaluation (10) but "peculiar" on the other hand is positive to neutral. The themes of each word also seem to clash with each other – one is about eventual failure while the other concerns uniqueness. Interesting right? Why would the author *choose* to put this rather ironic combination of words together?

If this all seems familiar, you're right! This is a lot like our "humanness" passage because once again we have a "half-known" opening sentence. So now what are you going to do? Yes! You're going to be curious about why art forgery is a "peculiar curse."

It's likely that the second sentence will be able to give us some guidance. Let's check it out!

In this sentence, the word "curse" (with its negative evaluation) links with "camouflage and deception" and "the believable lie" (this also has a negative evaluation). Aha! Now we're beginning to see why forgery can be thought of as a curse – because it relies on hiding and lies. But, there is also a slightly positive aspect to art forgery ("peculiar"). In the second sentence, the neutral to positive phrase "audacious and self-effacing" is the links to this word. Excellent! The "positive" side of art forgery is that it is both a bold and at the same time humble job.

Well done! You are well on your way to cracking the opening "half-known" sentence. Don't stop now – go on and read the third and fourth sentences.

Here we are introduced to the forger's world where to succeed he must be able to imitate something original. So at his very best, the forger could only paint copies, never an original – "imitations" versus "originals." This is indeed a peculiar curse because the forger will never be able to receive his glory because he can never take credit for his work!

Good work so far! You've done well disentangling those first couple of sentences!

Now I'm going to make a Table for the paragraph. A Table for a paragraph turns a jumbled mass of confusing sentences into something where you can easily find essential information.

Paragraph Table:

5	Art Forgery
10	—
15	Curse: imitating originals

Compare this Table to the summary sentence you wrote previously. If your summary sentence perfectly matches the above Table, good work! If your sentence doesn't, however, then you need to practice using this Table Method because it nicely dissects and summarizes the important elements of the Passage.

The principles behind paragraph Table are the same as they are for single words and sentences.

The topic (5) of this Paragraph is, of course, Art Forgery. The evaluation is negative since art forgery is referred to as a "curse" (I will be discussing the '10' of passages and paragraphs in more detail soon). The theme (15) is the central idea of paragraphs or passages. Remember – a theme gives us more information on the topic but in a summarized form. I'll discuss the detail (20) of passages and paragraphs soon.

So how would you summarize this Passage? Art forgery is a kind of curse because it forces the forger to always be imitators rather than originators. If we further simplified this, we'd be able to say it relates to problems and the difficulties forgers faced in their work.

If you looked at everything that's been said in the Passage, it all relates to the problems forgers face. "Problems" is my word. The author decides to be more severe and go with the idea that forgery is a unique type of curse that comes with many difficulties.

Side Note: the theme of a paragraph or passage can also be said to be a simplified version of the thesis statement. Finding the thesis statement is a skill you gradually acquire the more you read. The Table method provides you with a shortcut for identifying the thesis statement (look at the 15). In this paragraph, the thesis was hard to find because it's buried in the first (half-known) sentence.

Let's get a bit more practice in making a paragraph Table for the second paragraph at the bottom of Page 57.

Paragraph Table:

	Bottom Paragraph
5	
10	
15	
20	

After you've completed the Table try to answer this question:

Q: What is the main idea of this paragraph?

(A) The longhorned beetle was discovered in 1996 in New York State.

(B) The citrus longhorned beetle was discovered on an apple tree in October 2001

(C) To stop the citrus beetle people cut down healthy looking trees

(D) Normal environmental regulations were suspended because of the beetle

(E) Exotic pests are a growing problem

How did you do? Did you find it easy? Hard? Let's go through it!

Did you exclude (A) and (B)? Good! But why? You could've excluded them because the details they contained were wrong – in (A), New York State instead of New York City and in (B), October instead of August. Or you could have excluded them because they were overly specific.

I hope it was the latter! While all power to you if you were able to memorize all the supporting details from the paragraph and then use this knowledge to answer the question, this level of recall can actually hurt you on the SAT because you'll eventually get lost in the supporting details (20).

Did you exclude (C) and (D)? Great! Here the details are correct but they're merely supporting details. Remember? The question is looking for the main idea behind the paragraph.

Now you can see the danger of the details (20)! This is why I exclude details from the Table because they distract from our simplification process.

Paragraph Table:

5	Exotic pests
10	—
15	Growing problem (Answer Choice E)
20	Answer choice: A, B, C, D

The thesis here is: "Exotic pests…local ecosystem" (line 5).

From this point forward when you make Table for paragraphs or passages, don't include the detail (20).

Many students I've worked with mistakenly believe "beetles" is the topic (5) of this Passage. However, this isn't the case since exotic pests in general is the actual topic. If you read critically you can see that the beetles are just supporting details (20). This problem is similar to when we were discussing vocabulary (encircle, hound etc.) where many students got confused between the two concepts (15) and (20).

Make sure you don't make the same mistake!

If you'd found the thesis statement, this would have been no problem for you but sometimes the thesis can be tricky to find! Now I'm going to turn to how you can go about beginning your search for the thesis!

In the Paragraph on art forgery, finding the thesis was a challenge because there wasn't a clear thesis statement (because it was hidden in the "half-known" sentence). In this Paragraph on exotic pests though, there is a clear thesis. This makes finding the (5), (10), and (15) relatively easy as the thesis summarizes the thrust of the Paragraph.

Still finding your thesis hunt tricky? No problem! Keep in mind the three most common layouts for passages in the SAT.

Layout 1: The thesis statement is in the first line of the passage and is then followed by supporting details. For example:

> *John is an eccentric man* [thesis]. He wears a 19th century Puritan clothes to school, only eats cereal for dinner, and likes to sing songs from the 1920's when he's happy [supporting details].

Passage 1 on Page 57 is a good example of a paragraph that opens with a thesis and then provides supporting details.

A variation on this is when you have a long confusing passage. Here the author may decide to do you a favor and reiterate the thesis toward the end of the passage. The author does this because he wants to be sure you've grasped his main point and you haven't been misled by the supporting details.

Layout 2: There are supporting details and then a bit further on we have the thesis statement (as in exotic pests Passage). The thesis is generally within the first 30% of the passage. For example:

> He wears a 19th century Puritan suit to school, only eats cereal for dinner, and likes to sing songs from the 1920's when he's happy [supporting details]. *John is an eccentric man* [thesis].

<u>Layout 3:</u> Finally there is a looser passage structure with no clear thesis statement and a collection of facts and information just seemingly listed to support an overall point. For example:

Sarah highlights that John wears a 16th century Puritan suit to school, only eats cereal for dinner, and likes to sing songs from the 1920's when he's happy.

Steve, on the other hand, fondly remembers that when John celebrated his 16th birthday he gave presents to all his friends.

"If anything is currently popular, John isn't interested in it," was David's only comment about his friend John.

These are the diverse views about John.

Keep these different passage structures in mind as you read the passages.

Double paragraphs, Idea and Tone

Will our Table buddy be able to help us out when we look at double paragraphs? I bet you already know the answer – yes he can! Let's try it out on the two Paragraphs found on <u>Page 58</u> of the Blue Book.

Please read Paragraph 1 and fill in the Table 1 below. Good! Now read Paragraph 2 and fill in Table 2. *Don't* read both Paragraphs and then fill in the both Tables simultaneously. Instead, read the first Paragraph then complete Table 1 and then read the second Paragraph and fill in Table 2. The reason we follow this process is because if you try read both Passages and then fill the Tables in at the same time, you'll probably forget what you read in the first Passage.

<u>Double Paragraphs Table:</u>

	Table 1	Table 2
5		
10		
15		

Let's compare your Table to mine.

Double Paragraphs Table:

	Table 1		Table 2	
5	Literary Fiction		Literary Novels	
10	–	–	N	N
15	Self aggrandizing		For critics	

You've probably already noticed something different in this Table with the evaluation (10). The evaluation has been divided into the "tone" (on the left) and the "idea" (on the right).

Let's start off with the tone. Tone in writing isn't really that different from the tone of your voice. Ever heard the saying "it's not what you say but how you say it"? The same principle applies in writing. A definition for writing tone is: "the way the author expresses his attitude through his writing." Compare:

- "You think you're so pretty, don't you?"
- "You're so pretty!"

Which tone do you think is positive and which is negative? The first seems sarcastic and a bit derisive so the tone is negative. The second is clearly more approving and positive. The author's attitude is shown through his or her tone. We generalize tone into three categories positive (+), negative (−) and neutral (N).

The "idea" on the other hand is just a subjective evaluation of what is actually being written about, *e.g.* war (negative), love (positive), school (neutral – to some students – negative haha!), puppies (positive), etc.

Confused? No problem!

An easy way to understand tone and idea is to think of an article written about child abuse in an academic psychology journal. The idea is negative because of the terrible subject being discussed. However, the tone of the article is probably neutral because it's most likely written in the dry and distant way most academics write - scholarly, informative, and detached in tone or attitude.

What if the article was instead written by a survivor of child abuse? Then we would have both a negative idea and tone because it would be written in very personal, painful terms – incensed, resentful, tormented, etc. Check out the Appendix for a full list of tones!

Okay back to the good stuff and the double paragraphs.

Most of my Table is easy to understand but I need to highlight a few things. Let's start with tone and idea (since these are new concepts).

The key to finding tone is to look at the *interesting* nouns, adjectives, adverbs and overall structure the author has chosen. In Passage 1, the author contrasts the treatment of popular fiction (what he calls "genre fiction") to "literary fiction."

The author uses positive words to describe genre fiction – "*accessible*", "*fast-moving*", and "*unaffected*." This contrasts with the negative words he uses to describe literary fiction – "*self-conscious*," "*writerly*" prose. These interesting words should help you immediately get the sense that the author is not a big fan of literary fiction!

He continues this negative tone by highlighting that any literary fiction is always (*even* not "necessarily *good* literary fiction" – line 6) considered better than genre fiction and that literary fiction works dominate both newspaper reviews and short lists for awards ("It is these works and these works *only…*" – line 11). The author implies that this is an unfair situation. Therefore, the overall the tone of this Paragraph is negative!

The idea of the Paragraph 1, that literary fiction is overrated, is likewise negative.

How about in Paragraph 2? Here the tone is neutral because the author makes his case in a very matter-of-fact, objective way and there are no *interesting* words to signal a clear (+) or (−). The idea of Paragraph 2 is also neutral because the author simply lists characteristics of literary novels.

Side Note: when it comes to the double paragraphs/passages that relate to each other, often you'll have one passage that is relatively easy to understand and another more difficult. When you are creating the Table for the passages, use the information from the easier one to help you figure out what is happening in the more difficult passage/paragraph.

nging in the passages

You've done really well so far and now we're in the final stretch – the passage!

Please turn to <u>Page 60</u> in the Blue Book. Read Passage 1 and fill in the Table 1 below. And then read Passage 2 and fill in the Table 2. Again, don't read both Passages and then fill in the Table. Read the Passage 1, complete Table 1, read Passage 2 and then fill in Table 2.

<u>Double Passages Table:</u>

	Table 1		Table 2	
5				
10				
15				

Below is my Table for both Passages.

<u>Double Passages Table:</u>

	Table 1		Table 2	
5	Power of Silent Films		Mimes	
10	+	+	+	+
15	Engaging with the audience		Insidious influence on the audience	

Just like in paragraphs, if you're able to identify the thesis statement, your Table building process will be a lot easier (if you can't find the thesis statement it's not a disaster but it's something you should always keep an eye open for). In Passage 1, the thesis is "The silent film … make their imaginations work" (line 3) and in Passage 2 it's "Mime opens up…of a tour guide" (line 35).

Every paragraph has a purpose in the passage. Good writers don't include surplus info in their writing and they definitely don't include surplus paragraphs! As you read, interrogate each paragraph – why did the author choose to include this paragraph? What's its purpose?

Let's look at Passage 2 for example.

We already identified the first sentence as the thesis statement of the passage. So what's the purpose of the rest of the Paragraphs? These extra details all serve as support (through metaphor) for the thesis. What about the second Paragraph? This is an anecdote demonstrating the thesis statement. The third Paragraph contains greater analysis into why the author believes mime works insidiously to open up a new world to the audience. Finally, in the last Paragraph a stubborn audience member's unexpected pleasure is delivered as final proof of the way mimes bring pleasure to the viewer!

Can you see how the author faithfully constructed an argument by first laying the foundation (thesis) and then supporting it with a variety of paragraph styles (metaphors, anecdotes, analysis, example etc)? This is what you should be looking for as you read the passages.

Page 61 #19 of your Blue Book once again demonstrates the power of our Table buddy! Go ahead and try solving this question using our Table. I'll wait for you here.

Did you manage to match the information from the Table with answer choice (E) "Audience involvement"? You did? Great work! Answer choice (E) faithfully matches with our Table and links with the audience focus of both Passages.

Nice work! You're officially Table certified! ☺

Objective Reading

Objective versus subjective critical reading

You're out of the woods now, congratulations! Pat yourself on the back because you're able to find meaning in vocabulary, word pairs, sentences, paragraphs and passages. The final stop on our critical reading journey is to learn about objective and subjective reading.

Think about the SAT Game this way – a few points can make all the difference in getting accepted to a college. With so much at stake could ETS design a Game where the correct answers weren't 100% objectively true and the wrong answers weren't 100% objectively false? Of course not! If ETS did that they'd be sued by thousands of angry students who failed to get into the college of their dreams.

This knowledge is a powerful weapon to take with you into The Game!

Let this be your guiding principle when looking at every question in the SAT:

> <u>There is one objectively correct answer and four objectively incorrect answers in every question.</u>

There is no such thing as a partially correct or partially incorrect answer choice. Often you might find yourself thinking "Hmm...there seems to be two answers that are right here..."

Stop yourself immediately! Remember the guiding principle! It is impossible to have more than one objectively correct answer.

Why do I stress *objectively* correct?

The team that makes the SAT is not omniscient – they don't have perfect information on the author's intentions when he wrote a certain word etc. They are readers just like you who only have the text from which to base their questions! This means when ETS creates a correct answer they need evidence *from the text* to support the correct answer.

The SAT is an *evidence based Game*. This means all correct answers must be supported by objective evidence drawn from the text!

I love to tell the students a story about a commercial I saw on TV where the French president was brought news of a successful battle. The president looked thrilled and quickly asked the messenger "How did our valiant soldiers achieve such an incredible victory?" The messenger responded "We won because of Mreaa...!!"

Huh?

The reason for victory was clear as mud to me! Funnily enough, I wasn't alone. Some oddballs (with clearly too much time on their hands) had even started an online forum to discuss what on earth had been said! In this forum, people were going on and on about how they had perfect hearing, or that they'd watched the ad in slow-motion more than twenty times etc.

Eventually the company that made the commercial got so alarmed by the controversy that it forced the director of the ad to make a formal announcement; "Due to the unfortunate results of my ad, I would like to put on the record that the word was 'Mata Hari' (a famous sexy female spy during World War I) and sincerely apologize for any trouble I may have caused."

Haha!

What was the problem here? There were *no clues* leading up to "Mata Hari"! If they had previously mentioned something about how highly skilled French spies were, or that there are so many beautiful and sexy women in France, there would've been no problem figuring out the meaning of "…Mreaa" or need to issue an apology because the correct context would've been clear.

The SAT would also have to issue an apology if they created a question like this one! So relax and take a deep breath because you must be given <u>contextual guides</u> to ensure you're on the objectively correct path!

So what will you do during the exam? Always remain completely objective when reading, don't insert any of your own ideas, beliefs, or opinions into the text or the questions, and always be sure you have evidence from the text to back up whatever answer you choose.

Objective reading in action

You're probably thinking "Ha! This objective reading is easy! Of course I never insert my own feelings or opinions into what I read!"

Trust me – it's not as easy as it sounds!

Check out the following question:

If sound decision making involves both reasoning and instinct, then ignoring a person's instinct will _____ decision making.

(A) stop   (B) control   (C) manipulate   (D) distort   (E) divert

I've had students get angry when they hear the answer to this question because they believe the answer is "definitely A!" Other students will boldly and confidently assert that the answer is (B). Both groups of students are incorrect.

Why are they getting this wrong? Because they aren't reading objectively and aren't making sure they have evidence from within the text!

What is this sentence saying? To make good decisions, you need two things: reasoning and instinct. So what would happen if you ignore one of these?

If you ignored this contextual evidence, you'd be in the same situation as the people who watched the Mata Hari advertisement. They fell for their own *subjective* ideas about what "... Mreaa" was without having any contextual clues.

Before looking at the answer choices, think about what would happen if you limited one of the two things (instinct in this case) required for decision making? If you reasoned that your decision making ability would be changed or distorted, great! You're on the right track.

What is happening here? You've used contextual clues (reason and instinct are required for decision-making) and evidence from the text (instinct is ignored) to think of a possible answer. You've also done this in a very scientific, objective manner.

The formal definition of "distort" is to "twist or give disproportionate meaning to" – exactly what you're doing when you remove instinct from your decisions *i.e.* you're giving disproportionate meaning to reasoning and ignoring instinct.

Now you can see how being ruthlessly objective and drawing evidence from within the text can deliver the right answer to you every time!

Let's try another one:

Despite years of endless _____, leaders in the war-devastated nation kept striving for _____.

> (A) turmoil – talks
> (B) war – peace
> (C) chaos – well-being
> (D) disagreement – a truce
> (E) havoc – agreement

Again, your first impression was probably, "Hmm…there seem like a lot of answers that could be correct…"

Stop right there! Return to our guiding principle – there is only one objectively correct answer and that answer is…? Guess what? Only the objective pieces of evidence can tell us!

These pieces are: the words "war-devastated," "despite," and "endless". A war-devastated country would experience years of what? Well, all of the first column choices could work so what are you going to do now? Now you turn to your second signal – "despite!"

"Despite" tells us that we should be looking for opposites! There is only one answer choice that has a perfect antonym pair – (B). War is a perfect antonym for peace.

You'll notice the other word pairs that might *seem* like strong candidates for the correct answer aren't actually true opposites – it's just that their evaluations (10) are opposite (the word pair of "turmoil" with its negative evaluation and "talks" with its positive evaluation is a great example of this) so it seems as if they fit.

This is powerful objective reading in action!

What you should have learned from the above is that, simply put, being an objective reader involves using only the information that the author has stated. There is actually zero interpretation required because every single piece of information must be supported by what is in the Text.

Let's look at another example:

"If the true meaning of the Bible could be _____ and then remembered, I would be able to live like a saint."

(A) understood   (B) memorized   (C) learned   (D) noticed   (E) dug out

Again, let's read this objectively. Words that should immediately jump out at you are "true meaning," "Bible," and "remembered." The use of the word "and" signals that we're looking for a word that's roughly equivalent in some way (probably in evaluation or theme) to "remembered."

"Remembered" is a neutral word (10) that has a theme (15) of both "learning" and "understanding."

Now we have a problem – both (A) "understood" and (B) "memorized" could be answers. Both of these words could fit perfectly into this gap and the sentence would be completely correct!

This type of question will *never* appear in the SAT because why? There isn't an objectively correct answer!

Let's turn that sentence into an SAT style question:

"If the true meaning of the Bible could be *mined* and then remembered, I would be able to live like a saint."

Q: In the context of this sentence, the word "*mined*" most nearly means?

(A) understood   (B) memorized   (C) learned   (D) noticed   (E) dug out

It's the same sentence right? Wrong!

The difference is that the author in this sentence hasn't left any room for doubt. He's decided the exact word he wants to use "*mined*." You might be thinking, "Hmm. I think understood/memorized/learned is a better fit in this sentence…"

Woah! Stop yourself right there because we want to objectively judge what is written, not what should have been written.

Let's bring in our Table buddy for help in objectively figuring out the author's intention when it comes to the word "*mined*":

Word Table:

	Mined
5	Action
10	N
15	Extraction
20	e.g. removing valuable ore from the earth

Side Note: the Table forces you to be objective by providing strict rules to follow as you fill it in. You're not allowed to bring in subjective information because the Table is clear on what information it wants – nothing more and nothing less.

The Table makes our life easy. Where before we had two answer choices that could be objectively correct, we're now left with just one – "dug out." This is the only word that faithfully and objectively matches the theme of "extraction" – exactly the author's desired theme (15)!

This demonstrates why (A) "understood," (B) "memorized," (C) "learned," and (D) "noticed" *cannot* be the correct answer. Simply put, because they are not "dug out"! Answer Choices (A), (B), (C), and (D) *cannot* convey author intended meaning of mining and or digging out. This is why only (E) can be the only objectively correct answer.

This principle also applies to paragraphs. Let's look now at a paragraph.

Please read the paragraph and fill in the Table below:

"Over the past 50 years, many people have been advanced as the real author of Rousseau's works. Some sociology professors have even claimed that a shadow group of writers produced Rousseau's "The Social Contract" and many of his 15 other works. Other critics believe that a contemporary of Rousseau – Robespierre – was the true author of Rousseau's works. Laughably, the fact that Robespierre wrote all of his works on economics does nothing to repel those who would crown him the eminent political thinker of France."

Paragraph Table:

5	
10	
15	

Q: Which of the following best summarizes the main idea of this paragraph?

(A) Robespierre was an eminent economist of his time and wrote many excellent books on the subject.

(B) "The Social Contract" was an important book that allowed people to think of political sociology in new ways.

(C) Sociology professors agree that Rousseau was not the author of his own books

(D) Rousseau wrote many excellent books on the subject of politics and was a leader in the field.

(E) Robespierre must have written "This Social Contract" and many other works because he was a leader in the field of political thought.

There are a lot of details in this paragraph and you may be tempted to obsess over all of them. The key is to objectively simplify!

We have a lot of supplementary details here that support what?

Without simplifying, we'd struggle to stay objective in the face of so many details. What we need is a short, simple sentence that summarizes everything we've read.

Here's mine:

"Rousseau was good at politics and wrote a lot about it."

Paragraph Table:

5	Rousseau	
10	N	+
15	Political guru	

Only answer choice (D) faithfully and objectively adheres to this summary and our Table! This example illustrates both the power of summarizing and staying completely objective when you read a paragraph.

A well trained critical reader!

Well done! You've just completed a very important part on your journey to SAT Gaming success. The great thing about the critical reading skills you've just learned is that they're not purely for the SAT – they can be used on any critical reading you're likely to encounter in life.

This means to get a good SAT Critical Reading score you must read critically and only use information that the author's stated. This is true objective reading where instead of bringing in any subjective interpretation between the Text and the Answer Choices. Got it? Great!

Take a break and I'll see you on the next page for Micro Management.

PART IV MICRO MANAGEMENT-OPENING

Chapter Overview

We started our SAT Gaming journey by learning about the importance of having a commanding Macro-Management strategy. Then we talked about what it really means to be a critical reader and how to extract objective meaning from the text.

Now we're going to get our hands dirty!

Micro-Management is the scalpel to macro-management's chainsaw and eventually gets you SAT points you deserve. It's a collection of techniques we use to simplify and analyze questions, answer choices and the text.

This is a very exciting chapter where you're going to be learning a couple of handy tricks to beat ETS at its own Game!

Are you ready?

Then let's do it!

What does Micro Management Consist of?

SAT Critical Reading consists of four elements – the Questions (Q), Text (T), Essence (ES) and Answer Choices (AC).

Let's take a minute to chat about what the Text and the Essence are.

In SentCom, the Text is all the words that surround the missing word. In PBR, the Text is the entire passage/paragraph.

The Essence in both SentCom and PBR is evidence from the Text that allows you to objectively select a correct Answer Choice.

Huh? Let's explain the Essence another way.

Imagine you were only allowed to read the question prompt and the text but not the answer choices. After reading these two things, if you were then forced to write down your own answer to the question based on what you had read in the text, whatever you wrote would be the Essence! Think of a Student-Produced Response questions in the SAT Math section.

In some cases, the Essence is a single word directly from the text. In other cases, it might be your own summary of what you've read. Either way, the Essence is underline information taken from the text that helps you answer the question. underline

Let's look at two examples from the Blue Book:

Page 57 #2: Text – the entire paragraph. Essence – the word "imitation" (forgers don't get any glory from producing copies of originals) allows us to make a match with answer choice (B), "seek...another artist."

Page 44 Example (top of the page): Text – all words that surround the missing word in the sentence. Essence – the words "hoping to" and "compromise" (these words show us that a positive result was hoped for) and allow us to make a match with answer choice (E), "resolve... acceptable."

Don't worry too much if you're struggling with exactly what the Essence is, I promise you'll soon have lots of practice in finding it soon!

<u>The Questions</u>

Questions are guides in our search for the Essence, so we need to treat them with respect!

Imagine a seafood restaurant hires Captain Joe to catch exactly one tuna for their famous tuna dish. The owner of the seafood restaurant says, "Captain Joe! I want you to head out and catch me one and only one tuna – nothing else. If you bring me anything else, I won't be able to make my famous dish and you certainly won't get paid!"

If Captain Joe headed out to sea and netted tons of fish (along with a few tuna), would he have faithfully fulfilled the order of the seafood restaurant?

No.

Would he be paid?

No.

The order was specific – one tuna. Nothing more, nothing less.

In the SAT Game, you're Captain Joe and ETS is the seafood restaurant. ETS has given you strict instructions on what they want you to bring them (one tuna) and you must go out and catch that single tuna. Say you return with a tuna and tons of other fish? You failed. How about if you have two tuna? You failed. Half a tuna? Failed.

You get the point.

Bring ETS *exactly* what they're looking for. If you don't read questions extremely carefully, word for word you might find yourself catching the wrong fish!

Are all questions in the SAT the same?

No!

There are various types of questions, each wanting you to bring back a different type of fish. To be a good fisherman, you need to know what orders you'll receive and what type of fish you need to catch!

Let's begin our lesson by looking at the different types of questions you'll encounter in the Critical Reading section, what they're really asking for, and how you'll go out and find what they want in the text.

Question Type Diagram:

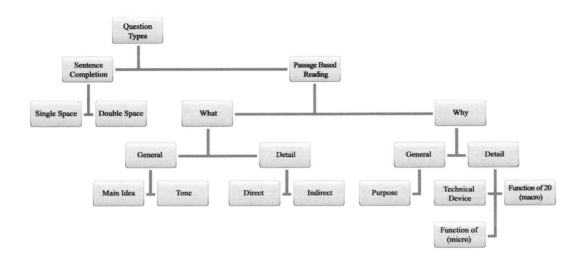

I'm not going to talk too much about SentCom questions here because the information they're looking for is obvious – it's the missing words.

PBR questions on the other hand are a bit trickier because they direct you to find different pieces of info from within the text.

PBR questions fall into two broad categories – *what* and *why* questions. "What" questions focus on parts of the Text where something isn't completely clear. There is a piece of the puzzle missing, and it's your job to look at the Text and find the missing piece of the puzzle. Examples of "what" prompts include:

- "What is the main idea of the Passage?"
- "In the context of line 26, the word "skill" most nearly means?"
- "In line 27, the author is referring to which group of scientists to support his idea?"
- "The author of Passage 2 implies that "kings with a capital K" are rulers that are?"

While "what" questions focus on creating clarity by finding the missing puzzle piece, "why" questions give you a puzzle piece and ask you to explain why it's included in the puzzle! Think of it this way: a passage or paragraph has been constructed in a certain way using a variety of rhetorical tools. It's your job to look at how the passage or paragraph was constructed and explain why the author chose to, for example, use a quotation mark, insert an unusual term or even write the whole passage. Examples of these types of questions include:

- "What is the main purpose of the above passage?"
- "The author uses the word "desperate" to convey what idea about Joe's circumstances?"
- "What's the function of the quotation marks in line 16?"
- "Why does the author repeat the word "frozen" three times in two different sentences?"

Now you should be able to divide all PBR questions into either "what" or "why" questions.

Overall General and Detail Questions

Let's move down a level and look at General versus Detail questions.

For a question to earn the label of "General," it mustn't reference any specific location in the paragraph/passage and it must not ask you to find any specific piece of information, which we'll call a "beacon."

General questions have no beacons because they're asking you to look at everything you've read and summarize it!

An example of a General question is Page 57 #1. Notice how it satisfies both requirements for a General question; a) the question relates to the entire paragraph and b) it doesn't ask you to find anything specific. General questions are usually either the first or the last questions on a section.

Detail questions on the other hand either directly reference a part of the passage or have a beacon for you to follow or find.

Line reference questions are the most obvious detail questions. Beacon-style detail questions are a bit trickier to find, but some examples can be found on Page 90 #11 and Page 91 #14.

Can you see that very specific beacons are given? In #11, we're asked to find *what* would be most crucial for the jurors to have order for Darrow to win his case. In #14, we're asked to find *the reason* Gabriel destroyed his ode.

Let's turn now to <u>Page 91</u> and categorize some questions.

- #12: a general question – it relates to the entire paragraph and has no clear beacon or line reference.
- #13: a detail question – there is a specific line reference (line 27).
- #14: detail question – there is a clear beacon; we're looking for "Gabriel's stated reason …"

<u>Side Note:</u> Where can you find the Essence for a question with no line reference? Luckily, ETS tells you where to begin your search! Detail questions appear in the order that their Essences can be found in the Text. Check this out – #13 deals with line 27 while #15 looks at lines starting from line 42. So our target for #14 is between lines 27-42. Sure enough, the Essence is drawn from "romanticism…a cloud of loving sentiment" in lines 28-29. Although there are a few exceptions to this guideline, this is a solid general rule for finding beacon-style questions that don't have line references. I call this the Essence Tracking Technique (ETT)!

- #15: a detail question – there is a specific line reference.
- #16: detail question – there is a clear beacon; we're looking for 'how Gabriel sees his father.' Let's apply our Essence Tracking Technique here. From the line reference in question #15, we know we're probably looking for information after line 43. Bingo! The Essence is "that criticism…important to me" from lines 50-51. Right where I predicted you'd find it!

You got it right? It's easy once you begin to practice! ☺

Nicely done, you've successfully managed to divide questions into "What" versus "Why" and "General" versus "Detail."

Let's move down another level.

90 James Hong

"What" Detail Questions - Direct and Indirect

"What" Detail questions can be further divided into "direct" or "indirect" questions.

How do we tell the difference between the two? Easy!

Direct questions have clear and obvious beacons to follow *i.e.* it's easy to see what information ETS wants you to focus on. Page 57 #2 is a perfect example of a direct question because we know exactly what answer the question requires: a definition of a "self effacing" **plus** the context of an act of art forgery.

Indirect questions on the other hand need a bit more analysis. Although these questions reference specific parts of the text, the link between the question and the text is still a bit hazy. These questions often contain wording such as "imply," "suggest," "assumes," "infer" etc.

#4, #5 and #6 on Pages 58-59 are examples of indirect questions.

Indirect questions often contain qualifiers (*e.g.* likely, best, and probably) in them. ETS inserts these qualifiers because, at the end of the day, they're also interpreting the text. By inserting qualifiers like "The author *probably* means X," ETS is protecting itself by saying "while this might not be *exactly* what the author meant, it's most *likely* given the evidence we have."

You might be thinking, "Oh interesting, there is room for interpretation here…"

Wrong!

As you learned in the last Chapter, there is zero interpretation involved in the SAT – all answers must have objective evidence drawn from the Text!

You must be disciplined when approaching indirect questions. There is no interpretation happening in these questions and you must never stray beyond what the question is asking and what is directly stated in the text.

Let's apply this to an example – Page 551 #12. We know this is an indirect detail question by the way it's asked ("suggest" + line reference).

Remember your Guiding Principle: all answers must be *fully* supported by the Text and not go beyond the borders created by the Text!

The Text states her father argued with the TV about a struggle. As a good critical reader you're probably asking yourself the question "What struggle?" Reading carefully, you'd see that "the struggle" connects with "struggling for civil rights" in the previous sentence.

Great!

Now we've got the borders set by the Text and also an Essence! Our answer should reference: i) her father ii) something about arguing iii) and civil rights. The only answer that fits within these limits is (C) "strong feeling…Civil Rights movement." All other answer choices deviate from within these set limits!

Another example of an indirect question is Page 914 #24. Let's follow the same process as in the above question. Read the question and then refer back to the lines around 55-65 and try find the Essence and correct Answer Choice. Please don't read the entire passage and just refer to the specified area of the Text.

What was your answer?

Here's a bit of a discussion on the way you should have approached the question.

The text states that "this cost Akaky…such an effort…he mopped his brow." This is our border – the answer choice must reference Akaky suffering in some way. The only answer choice that faithfully follows this is (E) "Akaky feared…"

You might be saying now, "Hey! To suffer is not the same as to fear!" Right! But remember in theme matching you need to be objectively expansive. In addition, since this is an indirect question your room to expand and interpret is a bit greater than it is for direct questions. "Akaky *feared*…" is the only answer choice that hints at Akaky's distress. This is why we can safely select (E).

"Why" Detail Questions

Detail "why" questions often use with the word "to" as in "in order to…," "is to," "used to…" etc. and are divided into:

- technical devices
- function of the 20 (Macro)
- function of the 20 (Micro)

First, Technical device questions look at small elements (quotation marks, capital letters, odd word combinations etc.) within the text and ask you to figure out why they were "allowed" into the Text. Page 59 #7 is an example of this type of question.

The second type of "why" detail question is what I call a "function of the 20 (Macro)." These questions are asking why specific details (20) are included in the Text. The reason? They're included to support the development of the topic (5), evaluation (10), or theme (15) of the overall passage/paragraph.

A good example of this type of question is on Page 61 #16. Here you're asked why a specific experience is discussed. The reason is because it builds on the overall theme (15) that the passage is attempting to develop (that mimes influence their audiences indirectly and subtly).

Page 489 #10 is another example of this "function of the 20 (Macro)". Try answering the question for yourself.

What was your answer?

Previous students of mine often chose (A) as their answer because they didn't understand the relationship between the supporting details, "they do no learn how to…book or magazine" (line 18) and the Topic Sentence, "Children spend….but…is nil" (line 17).These students somehow subjectively connected books and magazines with "traditional learning."

Imagine hypothetical incorrect Answer Choice: (F) Students don't appreciate the true meaning of the West.

Although (F) sounds similar to line 21 "They do not gain…West from…," it is still incorrect because it doesn't answer the question i.e. primarily serve to. This is a "why," not a "what" question.

If these students had realized this was a "function of the 20 (Macro)" question, they could've avoided line 18 (and 21) because they would've realized that they needed to focus on the Topic Sentence rather than the small details. The purpose of these "function of the 20 (Macro)" questions is to test your ability to differentiate between supporting details and topic sentences.

The final type of "why" detail question is the "function of the 20 (Micro)." Whereas the "function of the 20 (Macro)" is trying to influence the entire passage or paragraph's (5), (10) and (15), the function of the 20 (Micro) is looking at how small elements within the text influence each other. For example, how a specific word or phrases is used to further develop a theme.

> Text: "In my third year of college, I *embarked upon* an epic liberal arts study program."
> Q: The author used the phrase "*embarked upon*" to emphasize?

There are many other words the author could've used in this sentence, *e.g.* "started," "began," etc. However, the author chose "*embarked upon*" because it links with a Micro theme (15) of travel and exploration that he was attempting to develop.

Two similar examples can be found on Page 727 #19 and Page 984 #12.

A final note on "what" and "why" questions

ETS gets more bang for its testing buck by having some questions that include both "what" and "why" elements in the answer choice. In other words, you may face a "why" question but then see answer choices that include "what" and "why" elements. An example of this kind of question is Page 80 #7. You don't need to read the Passage or answer the question – just look at the answer choices.

The "why" question is focused on the purpose of the passage and covered in the first part of the answer choice (to explain, to refute, to propose etc.) whereas the "what" question corresponds to the second part of the answer choice (a situation, an argument, a change etc.) and simultaneously tests another aspect of your knowledge.

The Text and Essence

At the beginning of the chapter, I briefly laid out what the Text and Essence are (if you've forgotten, please refer back).

Before I explain more about the Text and the Essence, I'd like to introduce you to three people: Mr. Matching, Mr. No-Hope, and Mr. Choosing.

Mr. Matching is my idol and I want all of you to be just like him! This is how he approaches a question:

i) He reads the question to figure out *exactly* what info the question wants him to find (he pays particular attention to any beacons within the question in order to target the correct info in the Text);

ii) he refers back to the Text and finds the Essence that the question directs him to find;

iii) he writes the Essence next to the question;

iv) and he matches the Essence with the correct Answer Choice.

This method is *the* method of choice for attacking questions in the Critical Reading section because it's objective and applies a number of filters to prevent making wrong answer choices.

Mr. No-Hope is actually a very good reader. His successful reading abilities lead him to tackle critical reading questions like this:

i) He reads the question and then the answer choices;

ii) he *thinks* back to what he read in the passage earlier without referring back to the Text;

iii) and he selects the answer choice that matches what he remembers from the Text.

This is a terrible way of approaching the test! Don't ever use this method because you can't remember every detail in the text and have no filters to protect you.

Finally we have Mr. Choosing. Mr. Choosing (who could also be called Mr. Average because he uses the method most test takers use to solve questions) does the following:

i) He reads the question hastily and misses strong beacons in the questions;

ii) he refers back to the Text and absorbs *everything* he reads without regard to what is actually important;

iii) he moves back to the question, whispering a silent prayer that the answer choices will somehow help him find the correct answer;

iv) and he arbitrarily selects an answer that 'feels' correct with no solid evidence from the Text to support his selected answer.

Mr. Choosing often selects his answer choice by default, i.e. he eliminates as many answer choices as possible and then selects whatever is left. This is not objective test taking because there's no matching of evidence from the Text to the answer choice!

Mr. Choosing also makes trouble for himself by looking at the answer choices before he's got the Essence. In doing so, he faces the risk of being misled because many of the incorrect answer choices often include distracting information taken directly from the Text.

Whatever your current testing style is, I want you to become Mr. Matching!

I'm sure some of you are saying, "Hey! What if I read the question, read the Text and still have no idea what the Essence is! Can I at least now look at the answer choices for help?!" As a final option, you can refer to the answer choices for help but this is a desperate move.

Before you do this, I'd rather you used two techniques I'm about to discuss: Cherry-Picking and Top-Down.

Finding the Essence with Cherries

There are two methods you can use to find the Essence.

The first method is called the "Cherry-Picking." Being a good Cherry Picker is based on how well you can read critically. The greater your critical reading ability is, the easier time you'll have in trying to find a Cherry.

"What's a Cherry?" I'm sure you're asking.

Excellent question! A Cherry is something in the Text that helps you find the Essence. In some cases, the Cherry and Essence are exactly the same, in other cases they're different. The best way to understand what a Cherry is and see how it helps you find the Essence is to look at an example – Page 549 #3. Please turn to the Blue Book and try answering the question for yourself.

Using your critical reading skill you should immediately focus on two things – the colon (:) and the "and." A colon tells you that the information coming after the mark explains whatever preceded it, so in this question you can look for a synonym match in the answer choice.

So our Cherries are "blatantly proud" and "offensively bold." These are also our Essences, and we're going to be looking for a synonym theme match with these words.

Now it's easy to match our Essences to the correct answer choice – (D), "arrogant…. articulate".

Another example is Page 674 #12. Please turn to the Blue Book and try answering the question for yourself. Don't read the below until you answer this question first.

Here we can find our Cherry "mob" in the line 43. A mob is a large, disorganized group (Essence) which allows you to make a match with (B) Crowd.

Cool huh?

Side Note: I briefly mentioned the importance of "and" in the SentCom question. Words like "and" (along with others like so", "therefore", "because" etc.) are called 'Flag-Words' – they signal relationships within sentences. Please check the Appendix for a solid list of these Flag-Words (or combinations thereof) and what relationships they show. In the above example, "and" indicates that "blatantly proud" and "offensively bold" are similar in some way.

Your challenge as a critical reader is to Cherry-Pick information that's going to help you find the Essence. Let's try another example:

"The room was so _____ that the children complained of the high temperature and moisture"

        (A) Hot   (B) Wet   (C) Sultry

Can you spot the Cherries that lead us to the Essence? If you can, please underline them and answer the question.

The Cherries are "high temperature" *and* "moisture." You do need to be careful here though because these Cherries are working as a team to deliver your Essence. If you looked at only one Cherry you'd get the question wrong.

What do we have when there are high temperatures *and* moisture? Maybe humidity? Bingo! This is our Essence. Unlike in our previous example where the Essence and the Cherries were the same, here we had to use the Cherries to create our own *summarized* Essence of humidity.

The only answer choice that objectively matches humidity is (C), the correct answer.

Let's look at a PBR question – Page 58 #5. What would your answer be?

Can you spot the Cherries that will lead us to the Essence? If you highlighted "self-conscious" and "not necessarily *good*," then great job! What's the logic behind this?

Being a good critical reader, the phrase "literature with a capital L" should've made you curious because it's a half-known sentence. We know from studying critical reading that the author will soon provide information that'll explain this half-known sentence. This info will be our Essence since it'll explain what "literature with a capital L" is.

Our Cherries show this type of literature is "self conscious" and "not necessarily *good*" (notice the author uses italics for *good* to show how important he considers this fact). What do you call something that has "self conscious" and "not necessarily *good*" attributes? "Fake" or "pretentious" would be a good Essence here based on these Cherries. Only answer choice (B) "mannered and pretentious" successfully matches with this Essence. Let's see the formal definitions of "mannered" and "pretentious" to see how on target our Cherries and Essence were:

> **Mannered:** Marked by idiosyncratic mannerisms; artificial, stilted, and over elaborate in delivery.
>
> "pretending greater importance…than is actually possessed" = fake, pretentious
>
> "artificial" = fake, pretentions
>
> **Pretentious:** trying to impress by pretending greater importance, talent, or culture, than is actually possessed.

Great right? What you must see though is that I didn't do any magic! I just followed the method of Mr. Matching and used my critical reading curiosity do the rest.

It's that easy! ☺

Let's try a PBR question where the Cherry isn't the same as the Essence – Page 94 #29.

What was your answer? Also can you identify the Cherries that help you find the Essence?

Your Cherries   Your Essence:

Your identified Cherries should be "serious," (line 1) "simple but powerful," (line 2) and "made light of" (line 3). Here we need to create a summary word for the Essence (*e.g.* eminent, august, or predominance) as we did in the same way in our previous 'Sultry' example. This summary word allows us to make a match with (A) "dignified."

Finding the Essence using the Top-Down Method

I did tell you that there are two ways to find an Essence. While being able to find the Cherry is the preferred method, in some cases, you may simply be unable to find a Cherry.

In such a situation you're going to turn to the Top-Down method and try to find an incomplete Essence. Why incomplete? If we had a Cherry we'd be able to say what the topic (5), evaluation (10), and theme (15) are for a particular question, *i.e.* a complete Essence. However, because we don't have the Cherry, some part of the (5), (10), (15) puzzle is missing (in most cases, it's the (15)). So our Essence is said to be *incomplete*.

In Cherry-Picking, we were targeting certain words that would guide us to the Essence. In Top-Down, however, we don't have these words to guide us, so we have to rely *purely* on the Text. Can you see the difference? Cherry-Picking is *word* driven while Top-Down is more *context* driven.

Top-Down is basically about simplification and understanding how ideas are structured and presented. To fully explain Top-Down, let's turn to Page 37 #3.

I'm going to assume you've completely missed the Cherries for this question. The only thing you left to analyze is the Text.

What you're going to do now is create a Table that includes all Text that the question refers to. In the case of SentCom, it will be everything in the Text. In the case of PBR, it will be whatever portion of the Text the question refers to (this could be a sentence, paragraph or the entire passage).

Question #3: Table without a Cherry:

5	Research
10	N/+
15	??

I've included question marks in the Table above because if you'd figured out the theme (15) of this sentence, you would've been able to find the answer.

Top-Down gets its name from the way we use information in the Table to try find an incomplete Essence – we process information from the top of the Table and move down. Why do we do this? Because the topic (5) is usually the easiest information to find, followed by the evaluation (10).

This Table tells us the incomplete Essence is probably related to research (5) and has a neutral to positive evaluation (10).

As I previously explained, the Essence you get from Top-Down isn't as clear as the Essence you find using Cherry-Picking. However, this incomplete Top-Down Essence still adheres to our objective evidence standard and is still *far* better than Mr. Chooser's method of looking at the answer choices for help.

Using this incomplete Essence, we can eliminate answer choice (C) "sporadic" and (E) "problematic" (both these words have a negative evaluation). Nice! We've significantly increased our chances of getting the question right by taking these simple steps.

Your next step would be to insert the remaining answer choices into the gap for theme (15) and see which of them would fit the context that follows. Remember not the word that *feels* right but the word that *fits* right. If you inserted the three remaining words only (A) "comprehensive" would fit!

Top-Down might seem a bit unorthodox but it's based on solid reasoning. An author builds his argument using a topic (5), evaluation (10), theme (15) and details (20). These four elements aren't isolated ideas but work *together* to *make* up an argument. Therefore there is a relationship between the (5), (10), (15) and (20) and when you apply Top-Down, you're using this relationship to find the missing piece of the puzzle!

We'll have a lot more practice using Top-Down later when we analyze Test 1.

Top-Down with PBR

The main difference between Top-Down and Cherry-Picking is that Top-Down is time consuming and not as targeted and clean. Cherry-Picking is far superior if it can be done successfully but Top-Down gives you an emergency method to fall back on if Cherry-Picking doesn't seem to be working.

The key to Top-Down success is to be relaxed and systematic. Don't panic if you fail at Cherry-Picking – the answer is staring you in the face within the Text. You just need to step up and process the information properly.

Cherry-Picking is the only method to use during the First Round! Do not attempt Top-Down in the First Round because it'll soak up way too much of your valuable time.

Let's look at another example – Page 58 #5.

Here is your hypothetical Table.

Question #5 Table without a Cherry:

5	Literary Fiction	
10	–	–
15	??	

Let's apply Top-Down to this PBR question.

Once again, I'm going to assume that you found no Cherries and are stuck with just the raw sentences. I've Tabled the information from these lines in the above.

Here was my thinking as I built the previous Table. Let's start with what's easiest, what's the topic (5) here? Literary fiction. What's the idea (right side of the 10) – maybe neutral? The tone (left side of the (10)) is a little trickier. Let's read a bit further and see what evidence we can find. The author seems skeptical toward so-called "literary fiction" ("not necessarily *good*..." etc.). Let's go with negative for tone.

What incomplete Essence have we managed to find so far? We're looking for something about literary fiction (5) that has a negative evaluation (10). Let's see what happens when we turn to the answer choices.

Boom! You can immediately eliminate (A) "considered classic," (C) "unafraid to address," and (D) "successful" with their positive evaluations. You've just increased your odds from 20 percent to *50 percent*!

You're left with (B) "pretentious" and (E) "unfairly ignored." Here there is a slight variation from the technique we used to attack remaining answer choices after Top-Down in SentCom. Basically what we'll do now is compare pieces of answer choice (B) and (E) with what was stated in the Text.

Take a look at "book buying public" in answer choice (E). This phrase comes out of nowhere and has zero support from within the Text. On the other hand, "style" in (B) is exactly what the author has been discussing in the Text. (B) is our winner!

This is Top-Down in action. If you're still having trouble with Top-Down, don't worry! I've applied Top-Down to all the questions in Test 1, so you'll have plenty of chances to review the method there.

Simplification

A final tool to help you in your Essence search is simplification. Consider the following sentence:

> "To deny the life of architect Sir Herbert Baker its chief accomplishment is to reject the man his standing as the cause of at least sixty churches, twenty monuments, and a number of public spaces that, even if not a church survived, would still make him one of the greatest architects of his age, requires not only a massive conspiracy on the part of a generation of builders, planners and designers but also a very arrogant attitude towards educational opportunities."

This is a monster of a sentence that would strike fear into the heart of most SAT test takers! How on earth are we going to simplify this?

It's not that difficult to understand if you keep in mind that all sentences come with a Subject (basically who or what is doing something), a verb (what action is the subject doing) and an object (who or what is receiving this action). Let's look at a few examples.

Types of Sentences:

Type of Sentence	Simple Sentence	Complex Sentence
Example Sentence	Tom loves Jane so much	Tom loves Jane so much because she's warm hearted
Subject	Tom	Tom
Verb	Loves	Loves
Object	Jane	Jane
Modifier (if any)	so much	so much, because she's warm hearted

Can our huge Herbert Baker sentence be simplified in the same way? Yes! Here is how.

Herbert Baker Sentence Table:

Subject	Denying Baker is a great architect
Verb	requires
Object	conspiracy

See how easy that was? If you cut to the very core of complicated sentences and simply focus on the Subject, Verb and Object you'll make your life and your search for an Essence a lot easier!

Side Note: I didn't use any of the modifiers (the extra info that surrounds the Subject, Verb, and Object) to find the core of that paragraph.

The road ahead

Nicely done!

You've successfully navigated your way through Micro-Management – The Opening! You've learned many important concepts in this chapter including the types of questions you're likely to face in the Critical Reading section, how to efficiently and effectively search for the Essence, and a variety of tools to help you identify what's most important in the Text.

Take a breather. You're close to reaching the end of your SAT critical reading journey!

When you come back, we'll be finishing up with Micro-Management and learning how to Close with real power!

PART V — MICRO MANAGEMENT - CLOSING

Chapter Overview

This is the chapter where you're going to learn how to seal the deal and get points!

In the previous chapter, I discussed the Opening and covered three of the four elements in a Critical Reading section – the Questions (Q), the Text (T), and the Essence (ES). Now we're going to complete the quartet and look at Answer Choices (AC).

Why even bother to look at the Answer Choices in detail? It's simple. You may have understood the question perfectly and precisely extracted the Essence from the Text, but if you ultimately fail to select the correct answer choice, you won't get any points. The ability to select the correct answer choice is what ultimately puts points on the board!

Are you ready to go out and grab those points? Then let's do it!

Matching

We're going to dive right in with an example – Page 61 #16. Please try answer the questions before you move on.

What was your answer? Let's dig into the question.

Based on what we learned in the last chapter we can see that this is a "why" – "function of the 20 (Macro)" question. How do we know? The presence of "in order to" gives this question type away. In addition, the presence of the beacon "specific experience" signals these are supporting details, so instead of burying yourself in these complicated details you'll try and look for the Topic Sentence (which can be found in the previous sentence), "Audiences are… in context" (line 37-40). Simplifying this, we get an Essence of something like "audiences are sensitive to surroundings."

As our role-model Mr. Matching would do, we return to the Answer Choices and try finding a match to this Essence. Go ahead and try finding a match.

Are you having trouble matching? It's a hard question, so don't worry if you are. Try this if you're struggling: simplify each answer choice as much as possible (the fewer words the better). Can you find the correct answer now?

Here are my simplified Answer Choices:

(A) misconceive   (B) challenge   (C) intense   (D) unpredictable   (E) adjustments

If you're an expert critical reader, you'll be able to theme match "sensitive" (our Essence) with (E) "adjustments." This is a *very* tricky match to make (the definition of sensitive: quick to detect or respond to slight changes, signals, or influences i.e. make changes = adjustments).

What I'm trying to demonstrate here is that it's by no means guaranteed that you will be able to find the correct answer even if you've successfully analyzed the question and found the correct Essence. The greater the difficulty of a question, the harder it'll be to match the theme of your objective Essence with the correct answer choice.

Leveling up your theme matching ability

Let's look at a few examples of theme matching (ranging from easy to difficult):

- increase : escalate (1)
- faultless : impeccable (2)
- disagreement : incongruous (3)
- tacit : reserved (4)
- anachronistic : contradiction (5)

Can you see how the theme matches gradually become more difficult to find? Let's expand on this by looking at a few word pair combinations. Two of these combinations have themes that match and two do not. Try and figure out which is which:

- laconic…economical
- caricature …exaggeration
- peaceful… Sunday benediction
- contemptible … indulgent

The first two examples have words that are linked by theme while the last two pairs do not. Why? 'Laconic' is sparing in the number of words you use (either in speaking or writing) while 'economical' is the careful use of something. The theme link here is "sparing." In the second example, we've got the words 'caricature' and 'exaggeration.' A caricature is a depiction of something where certain aspects are exaggerated. Here the theme link is "exaggeration."

To succeed at matching, you need to do two things:

- have an *expansionary* sense of words (*e.g.* being able to see the link between laconic and economical) in order to see themes between the words
- be objective in your expansion of meaning so that you do not go beyond what the word actually means and create your own meaning.

If you can do both you will be an exceptionally good SAT test taker. If you're able to do the first but not the second you'll encounter the next problem…

Look at the third and fourth word examples ('peaceful..Sunday benediction' and 'contemptible… indulgent'). In these pairs, there is *no* theme link but many students mistakenly believe there is.

The reason? Students are going too far in finding theme links between the words. ETS tricks students by getting them to think something like this – "We're talking about a church on Sunday right? Ah then it must be peaceful!" Wrong. Those words are totally different. One is a blessing and the other means a calm state – the end! Any connection exists only in the mind of the test taker.

How about for 'contemptible…indulgent'? Theme match? Nope! These are words with a negative evaluation (10) but they are not linked by theme (15). The mistake many students make is they insert a "because" between the words (*e.g.* "the parent was contemptible *because* she was indulgent"). Can you see the problem here? The student has created a cause and effect situation where none existed. *Only* match! – Do not apply any logic or reasoning, just match!

Other matching problems

While difficulty to match themes is probably the most serious problem you'll face in matching the Essence with the Answer Choices, it's not the only one. There are three other problems

- Diction errors: you misunderstand what the word actually means because you're thinking of a word that sounds or looks similar. For example:

  rout...way

  ingenuous...creative

  discreet...separate

  eccentric...eclectic

  truncated...truculent

These are all incorrect matches. The list should instead read:

rout...defeat	OR	way...route
ingenuous...innocent	OR	creative...ingenious
discreet...prudent	OR	separate...discrete
eccentric...strange	OR	eclectic...diverse
truncated...short	OR	truculent...aggressive

- A lack of vocabulary knowledge: important words in either the Essence or Answer Choice are completely unknown to the student.

- A lack of precise vocabulary knowledge: the student knows basically what the word means but isn't 100% sure (or doesn't know alternate meanings of the same word). For example: are *discriminate*, *compromise*, and *relief* used correctly within these sentences?

  - The expert was able to *discriminate* between variations in tone.
  - He *compromised* his morality by taking a bribe.
  - The *relief* of the land was very uneven as we proceeded north.

These words are all used correctly! If you thought they were incorrect in the context, you probably don't realize the alternate meaning for the same word.

Take "discriminate" for example. The meaning most students have in their minds when they see the word discriminate is to judge someone unfairly based on their group or class *e.g.* racial discrimination. However, in the context of the above sentence, the word simply means the ability to see difference – something actually positive because it implies expertise.

In the second sentence, the word "compromise" actually means to corrupt oneself especially in terms of reputation. This is very different to the common definition of the word that relates to settling differences.

Can you see the point I'm making? The matching problem here comes from an imprecise understanding of the words.

You need to pay close attention to all four matching problems (themes, diction, weak vocabulary, imprecise vocabulary) as you search for matches between your Essence and the Answer Choices.

Matching can be tricky and it does take a lot of practice. Often the problem comes from either you being stuck with rigid dictionary style definitions or at the other end of the spectrum, you being too expansive in your theme matching.

If you're really struggling with matching, don't give up! Keep trying, keep reading and help is on the way! What I'm about to discuss will be very useful to those of you who are really having difficulty with matching.

<u>The Anatomy of Answer Choices</u>

Matching solutions – Single-Column

How do we overcome these matching problems? This is exactly what we're going to learn about in this Chapter and we're going to start off by looking at "Single-Column" questions.

A Single-Column question has one of the following characteristics:

a) a single blank question in SentCom;

b) a double blank question in Sentcom that we can solve by looking at only one Answer Choice column (either left or right);

c) a question where the Answer Choices are fundamentally different based on the topic (5), evaluation (10), and theme (15) of each Answer Choice.

Basically, a Single-Column question is a question where there is a glaring difference between each of the Answer Choices. For example, suppose we have an Essence of *Yellow* and the following Answer Choices:

(A) Red   (B) Black   (C) Yellow   (D) White   (E) Blue

This is a clear Single-Column question because each of the Answer Choices is fundamentally different. Or consider a paragraph :

The boy was admired for his great looks. The prettiest girl in the school wanted to date him and on Valentine's Day he got many letters from people in his class. In one humorous event, he was approached by a man on the street who asked him whether he wanted to become a model!

Q: What is the main idea of this paragraph?

(A) The boy is handsome
(B) The girl is pretty
(C) The girl is handsome
(D) The boy was not asked to become a model
(E) On Valentine's Day people exchange gifts with the people they love

Each of the above Answer Choices is fundamentally different so this is a Single-Column question. This is easy to see if we simplify our Answer Choices:

(A) Handsome boy
(B) Pretty girl
(C) Handsome girl
(D) Boy Model
(E) Exchanging gifts on Valentine's Day

The clear difference in the Answer Choices makes it easy to match with our Essence. If the Essence was "Good looking boy," it's a simple match, isn't it? This is the beauty of Single-Column questions – the obvious difference between Answer Choices makes matching with the Essence a lot more straightforward.

What you fundamentally need to understand and *know* in your heart is that all Answer Choices are *different*. This may seem a bit simplistic but it's amazing how many students fail to grasp this simple truth.

Often I'll hear students say "well there are two correct answers...?" Wrong! There's only one objectively correct answer! When you read and you find Answer Choices that seem to be the same, be angry with yourself for not being critical enough!

Same question, different Answer Choices

Let's develop this idea of fundamentally different Answer Choices a bit further. Check out the following example question and try answer it.

> The funeral took place after JFK was brutally _____ by a psychopathic gunman in Dallas, Texas.
>
> (A) assassinated   (B) murdered   (C) killed   (D) assimilated   (E) stopped

This type of question would never appear on the SAT because the themes in (A), (B), and (C) are too closely related and all of these Answer Choices could be correct.

In reality, every single Answer Choice in the SAT is completely different. Think of Australia and New Zealand, for instance. Their national flags look extremely similar but they are completely different countries. It is exactly the same in the SAT.

This is great news for the test taker because it means whenever you have Answer Choices that seems similar if you look closely they *have* to be different! With this as a guiding principle, you should know in your heart that every question can be viewed as a Single-Column question if you read critically enough.

So based on the above discussion, a more realistic cluster of Answer Choices for the prior JFK question would be the following:

> (A) assassinated   (B) advertised   (C) assisted   (D) accompanied   (E) stopped

Here the words are unrelated and each has its own completely different theme.

You need to realize that there is no 'could be' with (B), (C), (D) and (E) as potential answers – they are all 100%, completely wrong! Even if you have no idea what the word "assassinate" means you should feel confident in selecting (A) as your winner because none of the other Answer Choices match the Essence of "killing" (signaled by the Cherries "brutally," "funeral," and "gunman").

Matching solutions – Double Column questions

While Single-Column questions are our ideal, sometimes students encounter a different type of question: Double-Column questions. These are either:

a) Double blank questions in SentCom that can't be solved by looking at a single Answer Choice column (left or right)

b) Where there are two or more Answer Choices that seem to have a similar topic (5), evaluation (10), and theme (15), making it difficult to find an immediate difference between the various Answer Choices.

Why do Double-Column questions even exist? The reason is simple: they exist because of the reader's lack of critical reading ability. If the Essence from the Text is Yellow, the Answer Choices will look something like this for students with different critical reading abilities.

Difference in Student Perception's of Answer Choices:

Mid or Low Level	High Level
A) Yellowy-Red B) Black C) Reddy-yellow D) White E) Blue	A) Red B) Black C) Yellow D) White E) Blue

A student with an average to low critical reading ability will not see the differences in Answer Choices as clearly as a student with a high critical reading ability. Do you see the difference caused by the different critical reading levels and why now matching is so difficult?

Let's consider another example:

Text: The well-off South Korean cared about the plight of North Korean refugees.

Q: What is the main idea of this sentence?

(A) The South Korean was emphatic.

(B) The South Korean was sympathetic.

A high-level critical reader will easily discriminate between the Answer Choices. "Emphatic" relates to how you stress something (adjective form of "emphasis") whereas "sympathetic" relates to being caring. Lower level readers may confuse "emphatic" with the word "empathetic" (or even worse, "pathetic").

Another Answer Choice combination:

(A) He was empathetic.

(B) He was sympathetic

This combination type of Answer Choices will never appear in the SAT Game. Why? The difference in themes is way too fine to discriminate between the Answer Choices. A more realistic SAT Answer Choice combination would be:

(A) He was empathetic toward the plight of refugees from *North Korea.*

(B) He was sympathetic toward the plight of refugees from *Syria.*

(C) He was emphatic about disliking North Korean *leaders.*

You should be able to detect here how the shades of grey between the Answer Choices have been eliminated by the extra information, *i.e.* the refugees' countries "*North Korea,*" "*Syria.*"

The lesson here is this: keep in mind your critical reading ability when you're looking at the Answer Choices. If you see Answer Choices that seem the same, mentally change gears and dig deeper for the difference that *must* exist.

What do we do when we have Double Column questions that appear extremely similar?

Let's return to our JFK example with a slight twist:

"After JFK was brutally _____ by a gunman in Dallas, the entire nation_____."

Answer Choices Table:

Answer Choice	First Blank	Second Blank
(A)	assassinated	mourned
(B)	murdered	elated
(C)	killed	celebrated
(D)	donated	collapsed
(E)	advertised	cried

What is your answer?

If we'd only looked at the first set of answers ("assassinated," "murdered," "killed," etc.) this question would be impossible to solve. However, what allows ETS to introduce these closely themed words in various Answer Choices is the presence of a second word which renders the entire Answer Choice either completely correct or completely incorrect. Let's look at this in a Table.

Answer Choice Evaluation Table:

Answer Choice	First Blank	Second Blank
(A)	100	100
(B)	80	0
(C)	60	0
(D)	0	30
(E)	0	80

I've created a subjective measure of how well each word fits in the sentence for each Answer Choice. As you can see, we can quickly eliminate (D) "donated" and (E) "advertised" based on the completely incorrect left-hand column answer choice. Now we're left with (A) "assassinated," (B) "murdered," and (C) "killed." Since the left-hand column Answer Choices are too similar (hence this is a Double-Column question), we ignore them and focus our attention on the right-hand column Answer Choices.

The nation was definitely not happy after JFK was killed so we can eliminate (B) "elated" and (C) "celebrated," leaving us with our correct answer of (A) "assassinated…mourned."

Do you see what we did? Even though this was a Double-Column question, we *made* it Single-Column by finding the differences between the Answer Choices. This must be your mentality as you approach these Double Column questions!

Let's try another example - Page 37 #4. Please fill out the following Table with numbers that range from 0 (this word definitely doesn't fit) to 100 (this word is a perfect fit). Note: this is a completely subjective evaluation so don't worry if your analysis is different from mine.

Answer Choice Evaluation Table:

Answer Choice	First Blank	Second Blank
(A)		
(B)		
(C)		
(D)		
(E)		

Here's my subjective Table (FYI – you don't need to know how to draw this kind of Table. I'm just inserting it to help you understand the points I'm making.)

Answer Choice Evaluation Table:

Answer Choice	First Blank	Second Blank
(A)	100	0
(B)	80	0
(C)	100	100
(D)	0	0
(E)	0	60

(C) "requires"…"conform" is clearly the correct answer even though we *thought* there were partial matches in (A) "forces," (B) "expects," and (C) "requires" in the left-hand Answer Choice column and (C) "conform" and (E) "agree" in the right-hand Answer Choice column.

Let's look at a PBR example – <u>Page 393 #14</u>. Fill out the Table with your own subjective evaluations of fit just as you did previously.

<u>Answer Choice Evaluation Table:</u>

Answer Choice	First Blank	Second Blank
(A)		
(B)		
(C)		
(D)		
(E)		

I can create a Table for this question just as I did for the above example.

<u>Answer Choice Evaluation Table:</u>

Answer Choice	First Element	Second Element
(A)	0	0
(B)	0	0
(C)	80	0
(D)	0	0
(E)	100	100

The Essence we decided on is "skepticism to confidence." Starting with the left-hand Answer Choice column, we can easily eliminate Answer Choices (A) "fear," (B) "anger," and (D) "regret" because none of them match. This leaves us with (C) "uncertainty" and (E) "doubt." Turning to the right-hand answer choice column, we can eliminate (C) "despair." This leaves us with our correct answer of (E) "doubt...pride."

Are you beginning to see how to approach Double Column questions? There is a quick one-two punch combination:

1) Eliminate all Answer Choices that obviously don't match with the Essence.
2) Ruthlessly find the differences between seemingly similar Answer Choices.
3) Based on those differences eliminate and match!

Matching solutions – Trickier Double Column questions

The examples I showed you previously were straightforward, and after you *really* began to look critically at each Answer Choice, it was pretty easy to see the differences in the Answer Choices.

The real difficulty comes with longer PBR Answer Choices!

Let's check out an example:

Text: After a hard day's work, John wanted time to himself to think and mentally unwind. The beach was John's sanctuary.

Q: What was the author's purpose in writing this paragraph?

A) To indicate that the beach was a calming place for John after a hard day's work

B) To criticize the fact that John felt the beach was a silent place after a hard day's work

C) To portray the seashore as a calming place for John's father after a hard day's work

D) To illustrate that the beach was a idle place for John after a hard day's work

E) To emphasize that the beach was an interesting place for John after a hard day's work

A lazy critical reader won't be able to see the differences in the above Answer Choices. He'll either get lost because of the length of the Answer Choice or focus on correct information within the Answer Choice while ignoring what's incorrect.

ETS is aware that many students do this and so they change small things within the Answer Choice sentence to make it incorrect. Let's use a Table to deconstruct each Answer Choice.

Answer Choice Evaluation Table:

	ES	(A)	(B)	(C)	(D)	(E)
Why	Show	Indicate	Criticize	Portray	Illustrate	Emphasize
5	Beach / John	Beach / John	Beach / John	Seashore / Father	Beach / John	Beach / John
10	+	+	+	+	−	+
15	Soothing	Calming	Silent	Calming	Idle	Interesting
20	After a hard day's work	After a hard day's work	After a hard day's work	After a hard day's work	After a hard day's work	Before he started work

You've probably noticed something new in the previous Table – I've included the Essence! Another small difference is that I've also included the implied "why" question (*i.e.* what was the author's purpose, why was this paragraph written) in the Table.

You're about to see something beautiful.

Answer Choice (A) perfectly matches our Essence on every important measure – (5), (10), (15), (20), and "why." While this is a good thing to see, the really potent part of the Table comes next.

Remind me what the Essence is again? It is objective evidence taken from the text that allows us to make a match with the correct answer (I hope you're screaming this out). So if *anything* doesn't match this Essence that Answer Choice is immediately disqualified!

Let's follow this logic to its conclusion. In (B), the "why" (criticize) doesn't match with our Essence "why" (show). Likewise, the theme (15) of "silent" doesn't match the Essence theme of "soothing," so (B) is eliminated! We can follow the exact same process for the rest of the Answer Choices and easily eliminate the rest of the Answer Choices based on the fact that they don't match the Essence.

Cool huh? Even the most stubborn Double-Column question can be attacked in this manner.

Counterbalancing

What I've described above is known as "counterbalancing." Counterbalancing is the predictable way ETS constructs its Answer Choices. Every incorrect Answer Choice on the SAT will have its topic (5), evaluation (10), theme (15), details (20), or even a combination of these not matching the Essence. You can see this in our previous Table. Every incorrect Answer Choice has some mismatch between it and the Essence.

This should boost your confidence because now you have a way to attack these longer PBR Answer Choices – by digging into their topics, evaluations, and themes!

Let's prove it – Page 765 #15. Try answering the question and fill in the Table on the next page.

Answer Choice Evaluation Table:

	ES	(A)	(B)	(C)	(D)	(E)
Why						
5						
10						
15						
20						

Answer Choice Evaluation Table:

	ES	(A)	(B)	(C)	(D)	(E)
Why	Show	Point Out	Suggest Disapproval	Indicate	Express approval	Show outrage
5	Adams / Wife's point	Adams / Issue	Issue	Adams / Wife's point	Adams / Issue	Adams / Wife's Request
10	+	+		+	+	z
15	Considered	Desire to solve	No time devoted	Glimpsed	Respond	Dismiss
20	Not be taken seriously, if enacted… our masculine systems.	Immediate, pressing	Any, insignificant	Despite his cultural limitations	Swift, crucial	Outright

We have a strong Essence and are ready to tackle each of the Answer Choices with our handy comparison Table. Although we've already made the appropriate eliminations, for the sake of discussion, assume that this Table was unmarked.

At this stage, we obviously want to retain all Answer Choices that seem to match our Essence *and* eliminate Answer Choices that don't.

A highly critical reader will see this question as a Single-Column question (*i.e.* all answer choices are clearly different and there is a clear difference between the Answer Choices) and quickly eliminate four Answer Choices and match with the correct Answer Choice. A reader with lower ability will not be able to eliminate 2 or 3 (let alone 4) Answer Choices because he believes they match the Essence or he doesn't understand them.

Side Note: The number of Answer Choices you're able to discard is related to your critical reading level. When you're on the fence between retaining and eliminating (or if you don't understand) an Answer Choice, fall on the side of keeping it.

Let's return to my Table.

Take a look at Answer Choices (C) and (D). These two Answer Choices are so similar that many students will probably classify this question as Double-Column. Why? The difference in the (5), (10), and (15) is extremely slight.

Let's look at this question through the eyes of a student with limited critical reading ability. Assume he was able to eliminate (A) and (E) in the First Round and is returning to this question in the Second Round.

Well-trained in the art of attacking a Double-Column question, this student would create a comparison Table for the remaining Answer Choices to compare with the Essence.

Answer Choice Evaluation Table:

	Essence	(B)	(C)	(D)
5	Adams / Wife's point	Issue	Adams / Wife's point	Adams / Issue
10	+	—	+	+
15	Considered	No time devoted	Glimpsed	Respond

Why wouldn't our student include the "why" or details (20) in their Table? Because he has read critically, there will be a difference within the topic (5), evaluation (10), and theme (15). The "why" is not included because it examines motivations (something that can be subjective and confusing). We rather stick with what's obvious and can be objectively matched: the topic (5), evaluation (10), and theme (15).

Our theoretical student would be able to eliminate (B) pretty quickly because the evaluation (10) and theme (15) of this Answer Choice don't match our Essence. You're probably wondering why he wasn't able to eliminate (B) in the First Round? The reason is he wasn't reading critically enough in the First Round and the Table has *forced* him to read the Answer Choices more critically in the Second Round.

He is still left with (C) and (D) though. To me, there is a difference in the (15) but I guess a lower level student wouldn't be able to tell the difference between a theme of "glimpsed" and "respond" (something a higher level reader would have no problem with) and would probably think they both matched with the Essence of "considered."

This student has actually done pretty well – he's successfully found an Essence and eliminated three Answer Choices! What should he do now? He must find a difference between the Answer Choices for *Closing*!

If he can't find any differences between the Answer Choices, he'll never be able to find a match with Essence. Put simply, he must change this Double Column question into a Single-Column question!

What's left in each Answer Choice that could help us find the difference between (C) and (D)? Obviously it's the "why" and the details (20) – the difference between the Answer Choices must found here.

My student must now decide which element (the "why" or details (20)) would be easiest to compare. Which element do you think would be easiest to compare? I'm guessing you'll probably compare the "why" because there is an obvious difference between "indicate" (show) and "express approval" (agree with) – a clear-cut, black and white comparison.

After making this decision, the student would return to the Text and see if he can find objective evidence to support either "indicate" or "express approval." Which of these elements does he evaluate first? Whichever looks like Brad Pitt!

Huh?

Meet Brad Pitt, another SAT Test-taking Technique buddy

Let's say you walk into a big party filled with total strangers. You don't know anyone's name and even if you were quickly introduced to a few people, you'd probably quickly forget their names by the next day because everyone was pretty much the same.

Now imagine you walk into party filled with total strangers and Brad Pitt! Do you think you'd be able to remember anyone who was at the party the next day? Of course – Brad Pitt!

The Double-Column Answer Choices (C) and (D) are your room of strangers – you need to find Brad Pitt! This is the outstanding detail that you can point to and compare with all other details.

"Express approval" is a big, clear Brad Pitt that we can compare to the Text. "Indicate," on the other hand, is more bland and difficult to target – an average person you'd meet at the party. Returning to the Text, it's impossible to find any "expressions of approval." Thanks to Brad Pitt, we can eliminate (D), leaving us with our correct answer of (C).

If my student somehow felt more confident about comparing the details (20) of both answer choices (C) and (D), then he would apply Brad Pitt to the details (20).

The phrase "swift" and "crucial issue" are prominent Brad Pitts that we can evaluate against the Text. Is there any support in the Text for "swift" and "crucial issue"? None! "Swift" means to move quickly whereas "for an instant" means to take virtually no time.

By the same token, "crucial issue" is in fact, the opposite to what is stated in the Text - "trivialized her argument" and "could not be taken seriously." Great! We know that if *any* part of the Answer Choice is wrong, the entire Answer Choice is wrong so we can safely discard (D).

Now you're well armed for tackling seemingly correct Double-Column questions!

Answer Choice Selection

The above discussion was based on two pretty big assumptions: a) you had a very clear Essence and b) any difficulty you had in matching came from your inability to find differences among the Answer Choices.

In the real world, things are more complicated. Maybe your Essence is not perfect. Or maybe you can't find any differences among the Answer Choices. Or maybe there are words in the Text or Answer Choices that complicate the matching process. What are you going to do then?

Don't worry. Now you've got James Hong! ☺ I have a few tricks to help you out!

Unclear matching

Imagine a machine that could measure how sure a student felt that a particular Answer Choice matched his Essence. The machine would give a reading that ranged from 100 (perfect match) to 0 (definitely doesn't match) for each answer choice:

(A) 70   (B) 60   (C) 0   (D) 0   (E) 0

What would be your approach here? If you're like the majority of students you'd simply choose (A) since this Answer Choice 'feels' the most correct with a reading of "70." This is the *wrong* approach!

What you should've done is proceed with caution and fully admit to yourself that you've made an error. What error? You've failed to find the *one* objectively correct Answer Choice and exclude all the objectively incorrect Answer Choices! Your 'feelings' don't meet the requirements for an *objectively correct* Answer Choice match.

Let's see how this plays out in a few examples based on the following question – "Microsoft is a _____ company: it arouses fear in many of its competitors."

To guide you in examining this question, I'll use the following notation:

- 'O': An Answer Choice we believe objectively matches our Essence
- 'X': An Answer Choice we believe does not match our Essence
- 'Δ': An Answer Choice we believe could match with the Essence but we still feel there's something problematic about the match
- '?': An unknown Answer Choice where we don't understand the meaning

Please choose your own answer for each scenario, using the same notation. You can fill in your answer between the ' '

Answer Choice Scenario 1:

(A) gentle – '__' (B) comedic – '__' (C) silly – '__'   (D) caring – '__' (E) impetuous – '__'

Answer Choice Scenario 2:

(A) gentle – '__' (B) comedic – '__' (C) unbeatable – '__' (D) silly – '__' (E) impetuous – '__'

Answer Choice Scenario 3:

(A) gentle – '__' (B) comedic – '__' (C) unbeatable – '__' (D) silly – '__' (E) impetuous – '__'

Scenario 1: four 'X' versus one 'Δ'

Let's assume that (E) "impetuous" is a 'Δ'. Even though we're sure the other Answer Choices are incorrect, we can't automatically select (E) as our winner yet because of the presence of a 'Δ'. In the Second Round we'd have to double check that we're 100% certain that the other four Answer Choices are 1 00% incorrect and only then can we select (E) as our answer.

Scenario 2: O and 'Δ'

If you're an excellent critical reader, you'd probably easily eliminate all Answer Choices but (C) "unbeatable." A lower level critical reader would probably feel (C) is an 'O' but would still feel uncertain because (E) is a 'Δ'or '?'.

What should we do? Right! Return to the question in the Second Round!

In the Second Round, we'd first need to step back, take a breath, and remind ourselves that each Answer Choice is completely different! Next we need to ask ourselves a question: which of these words am I most familiar with?

In this question, "unbeatable" is probably more familiar to you. So insert it into the blank and see if it fits. If you find it does, great – that's your winner! For the sake of illustration, suppose you were more familiar with the word "impetuous" rather than "unbeatable." Again, you'd insert "impetuous" into the blank and probably find that there wasn't a solid match because "impetuous" means "acting quickly without thought or care." Now you'd need to have the courage to select "unbeatable" as the answer even though it was not as familiar as "impetuous" is to you!

What I did in this scenario was *force* a showdown between the Answer Choices so it's no longer a battle between "degrees of correctness." Rather, there is a black and white decision.

Scenario 3: '?' and 'Δ'

In this scenario, you have no idea what (C) "redoubtable" – '?' means and (E) "impetuous" – 'Δ' rings a bell for you somewhere in your mind.

So what are you going to do here? Again you're not allowed to simply choose "impetuous" because it's more familiar to you. You need to check that it objectively fits! If it doesn't do so

perfectly (that little voice in your head is warning you very clearly), you need to step back from "impetuous" and boldly go with the unfamiliar i.e. "redoubtable" which means unbeatable.

Getting your psychology and system right

The above scenarios all illustrate the same overarching principle – going by "instinct" or "gut-feel" is a sure way to slip in the SAT. The *only* way you can beat ETS and your subjective feelings is to ignore your instincts and:

- admit you're wrong, not the Answer Choices.
- identify what you *truly* know before you make any judgment call on what is correct and incorrect.
- watch out for the problematic familiar 'Δ'and listen to the warning *voice* in your head.
- follow a rigorous system rather than your instincts.
- have the *courage* to take a chance on an unfamiliar Answer Choice.

Our previous examples all covered Single-Column questions. Double-Column questions have these matching problems too, of course. Consider the following Marking Map:

(A) O … X

(B) X … O

(C) X … Δ

(D) X … ?

(E) ? … X

How do we go about handling this?

The first technique you'll use is known as the "Bottom-Line" approach. Bottom-Line is a technique that's used to find the "soul" of an Answer Choice by simplifying it to the greatest extent possible.

Try getting the Essence out of this Text:

"But what seemed most amazing to me was how I endured the endless problems that came with being the youngest child."

What's the match to the following Answer Choices (do your own '?', 'O', 'X', and 'Δ' markings next to each Answer Choice).

Answer Choice Marking Table:

Answer Choice	Your Marking
(A) impartial	
(B) remorse	
(C) awe	
(D) pride	
(E) rage	

Here are the markings I believe various kinds of students would make based on their critical reading abilities.

Answer Choice Marking Table:

High Level	Moderate Level	Low Level
(A) X	(A) X	(A) ?
(B) X	(B) X	(B) ?
(C) O	(C) Δ or O	(C) Δ or O
(D) X	(D) Δ or O	(D) Δ or O
(E) X	(E) X	(E) X

A student with a moderate critical reading level will see (C) "awe" and (D) "pride" as most likely. Let's put ourselves in his shoes. We're now going to try simplify these Answer Choices further and find the *soul* of each Answer Choice (*i.e.* Bottom-Line them). Here are ours:

(C) amazed! (D) confidence

Now can we find a match? Easy huh? This is the strength of simplifying and finding the soul of an Answer Choice through the Bottom-Line. Answer Choices that seem like they could both fit the Essence are revealed to be totally different and not even a close match!

Another method we could use is 'Antonyms.' With Antonyms, we're trying to find differences among Answer Choices by thinking of the opposite. For example, the opposite of "pride" is "shame" while the opposite of "awe" is "indifference." If these words were close synonyms they'd have a similar antonym. What's an antonym for "amazed"? "Disappointed" – which closely matches with "indifference." Bingo! By examining antonyms, it becomes easier to see the differences among the Answer Choices.

Let's shift focus and look at this question through the eyes of a low level student. Now we're stuck with (A) "impartial," (B) "remorse," (C) "awe," and (D) "pride." Since we have no idea about (A) and (B), we'd have to leave these Answer Choices aside for now. Our only hope lies in a successful Bottom-Line and match with (C). Failing this, we'll just have to take a guess and hope for the best! Either that or IMPROVE YOUR VOCABULARY POWER!!

More Bottom-Line

Let's try a few more Bottom-Line examples (assume an Essence of "*private illustrations*"): What's the match to the following Answer choices? Make your own '?', 'O', 'X', and 'Δ' markings next to each Answer Choice.

Answer Choice Marking Table:

Answer Choices	Your Marking
(A) subjective qualification	
(B) memorable observations	
(C) personal depictions	
(D) informal analysis	
(E) objective identification	

Potential markings:

High Level CR	Moderate Level CR
(A) X	(A) ?
(B) X	(B) Δ or O
(C) O	(C) O
(D) X	(D) Δ or O
(E) X	(E) X

A student with a moderate critical reading level will probably be torn between either (B) "memorable observations," (C) "personal depictions," or (D) "informal analysis." Again, let's have a look at things from his perspective and Bottom-Line the Answer Choices to find a point of difference.

Side Note: always start your Bottom-Line by looking at the word that's being modified rather than the modifier.

Here's my Bottom-Line (I've done all of the Answer-Choices for illustrative purposes):

Answer Choice Bottom-Line Table:

	Private Illustrations
(A)	Exception
(B)	Watch
(C)	Show
(D)	Measure
(E)	Difference

The only Bottom-Line that matches with "illustrations" (the modified portion of the Essence) is (C) "show."

Let's turn to a slight variation on the above example. You'll notice two of the Answer Choices have been altered (I'm assuming the same Essence as before – "private illustrations"):

(A)   subjective qualification

(B)   memorable observations

(C)   personal depictions

(D)   formal portrayals

(E)   objective identification

The tricky part of this Answer Choice combination is on the right-hand side of Answer Choices (C) and (D), "depictions" and "portrayals." Even after we have tried to Bottom-Line each Answer Choice, the two words are too similar for even the best critical readers to differentiate and both seem like an objective match. The right-hand side visually:

Answer Choice Marking Table:

Answer Choices	Your Marking
(A)...qualification	?
(B)...observation	Δ
(C)...depictions	O
(D)...portrayals	O
(E)...identification	X

(A) ...qualification – '?'
(B) ...observation –'Δ'
(C) ...depictions – 'O'
(D) ...portrayals – 'O'
(E) ...identification – 'X'

We cannot eliminate (A) "... qualification" nor (B) "... observations" at this stage because there's no evidence that allows you to X them. However, when you have a synonym pair like in (C) "depictions" and (D) "portrayals," it's highly likely you have the correct answer within these Answer Choices!

What's our next step? Can you guess? If you said we need to Bottom-Line the modifiers (left-hand side of the Answer Choices) and attempt a match you're totally correct! If we do this, we're left with the following marking map.

(C) personal ... depictions : 'O' ... 'O'
(D) formal ... portrayals : 'X' ...'O'

Now there is no mystery about which answer is correct – (C) which has matches in both the left and right-hand Answer Choice columns.

Confusing Essence

Interestingly enough, Double-Column questions can actually be helpful in situations where you've got no idea about the Essence. See for example Page 37 #4. Try to complete the following Table.

Answer Choice Marking Table without Essence :

	Left Column	Right Column
Essence	?	?
(A)		
(B)		
(C)		
(D)		
(E)		

Assume for this question you have no Essence at all. What do you notice about the Answer Choices? (A) "forces" and (C) "requires" have close synonym pairs in their left-hand Answer Choice column and (C) "conform" and (E) "agree" have close synonym pairs in their right-hand Answer Choice column. The overlap in synonym pairs strongly suggests that (C) is the correct answer (which it is!).

Another example can be found on Page 549 #3. Try and solve this question by only looking at the Answer Choices. Can you do it? Try to complete the following Table.

Answer Choice Marking Table without Essence:

	Left Column	Right Column
Essence	?	?
(A)		
(B)		
(C)		
(D)		
(E)		

Answer Choice Marking Table without Essence:

	Left Column	Right Column
Essence	?	?
(A)	haughty	impudent
(B)	irresolute	insolent
(C)	presumptuous	loquacious
(D)	arrogant	articulate
(E)	reverential	contemptuous

If you faithfully applied the technique I showed you, you should be able to see that (A) "haughty…" and (C) "presumptuous…" are synonym pairs and (A) "…impudent" and (B) "…insolent" are also synonym pairs, so (A) is the answer because we have a synonym pair overlap. Great right?

Even if you're only able to find either the left or right hand column synonym pair, you'll have a 50/50 shot at getting it right. If you want to increase your odds of getting the question right even further, select the Answer Choice that contains the more difficult vocabulary word (in #3 it's "haughty" versus the easier "arrogant" and in our previous example of Page 37 #4, it was "conform" versus "agree"). Resist your instinct to automatically go with the familiar easier word.

A signal from the Answer Choices

Look at the following Answer Choices and try match them to an Essence of "private illustrations" (let's assume this was the Essence you got from the Text). Here are the Answer Choices:

	Left Column	Right Column
Essence	private	illustrations
(A)	disinterested	qualification
(B)	memorable	observations
(C)	impersonal	depictions
(D)	informal	performance
(E)	objective	identification

Please choose your own answer and make your own markings on the following Table with '?', 'O', 'X', and 'Δ'.

Answer Choice Marking Table:

	Left Column	Right Column
Essence	private	illustrations
(A)		
(B)		
(C)		
(D)		
(E)		

After doing our Bottom-Line and following all the steps we outlined previously, we're left with the following Marking Map. Can you see the problem?

Answer Choice Table with the Problematic Essence:

	Left Column	Right Column
Essence	private	illustrations
(A)	disinterested	qualification
(B)	memorable	observations
(C)	impersonal	depictions
(D)	informal	performance
(E)	objective	identification

There is no clear answer. Why? The reason lies in the Essence. The hypothetical Essence I said you found ("private illustrations") is incorrect!

Now we're going to learn what you can do to overcome a situation where you have the wrong Essence. First – don't panic! This confusing marking map is a friend, not an enemy. Your friend is warning you that you've gone astray somewhere in the process and should make a correction!

So we need to go back and figure out where we went wrong. To do this, we need to change gears a bit and acknowledge a new truth about the Essence: information in the Essence doesn't have equal importance when we match. The (5), (10), and (15) in that order are king!

This concept is called "the Hierarchy of Importance."

Consider an Essence of "John swallowed his toothbrush and died" and Answer Choices of:

(A) John was injured while brushing his teeth.

(B) John died in a car accident.

Which of the following Answer Choices matches with our Essence? Neither of them right? So we're being warned that something is wrong! Suppose you tried to find the correct Essence and failed, then you'd be stuck with what you have. Let's Table this incorrect Essence.

Answer Choice Table with the Problematic Essence:

	Essence	(A)	(B)
5	John	John	John
10	–	–	–
15	Died	Injured	Died
20	Brushing his teeth	Brushing his teeth	Car accident

Let's start with the most important info (5). Both Answer Choices discuss John so we can't eliminate anything yet. Similarly, both have negative evaluations (10) so we can't eliminate here either. What about when it comes to the theme (death)? Only one Answer Choice (B) faithfully matches this, so we'd select this as our answer.

You might say "Hey! The Essence never said John died in *a car accident (20)*!" – correct and this is exactly the point. These details are where you probably made the original mistake so forget them and focus on the "Hierarchy of Importance" – the topic (5), evaluation (10), and theme (15) of the Essence!

In the Table for (A), the theme (15) is incorrect while in (B), the detail (20) is incorrect. So what do we do? Simple! We follow the Hierarchy of Importance and select (B) since its (15) is correct, unlike (A).

Let's apply this strategy to the above "private illustrations" question. If we applied our Hierarchy of Importance, we'd focus on "illustrations," ignore the "private" part of the Essence (since this is just a modifying detail *i.e.* (20)) and then see which of our Answer Choices faithfully adheres to *only* this element of the Essence. In this case, only (C) "depictions" matches with "illustrations."

Now we're going to apply the Hierarchy of Importance to a real question: <u>Page 489 #14.</u> Assume we couldn't find any Essence here and just need to work with what we have – "attempts at the latter." Suppose we know this is about an "attempt" (5) and this is negatively evaluated (10). So we have the following Table.

<u>Incomplete Essence Table:</u>

	Essence
5	Attempts
10	?
15	??

With this Table giving us the incomplete Essence, we're now going to turn to evaluating it against the Answer Choices.

<u>Answer Choice Marking Table with the Incomplete Essence:</u>

	Left Column	Right Column
(A)	unpolished	products
(B)	unpopular	changes
(C)	misunderstood	creations
(D)	ill-conceived	failures
(E)	foolish	imitations

Can we find any Answer Choice that seems to have a connection to our incomplete Essence? Remember, we look at the right-hand column of the Answer Choice (at what is being modified). There is only one Answer Choice that comes close to a negatively evaluated theme of "attempts" – (D) "failures." You probably noticed that that "misunderstood" is close to "ill-conceived," but this point is moot since "creations" easily makes this potential Double-Column question a Single Column one.

Great huh? Even with our extremely weak Essence we could use the Hierarch of Importance as a guide!

Let's summarize our approach for evaluating Answer Choices that appear similar:

i) we have to find a difference! Start by using Bottom-Line or Antonyms Approach. If this fails and they still look similar, you're dealing with a...

ii) Double-Column question. Since this is a Double-Column question, you'll be faced with Answer Choices that *seem* similar but we know they're *actually* different. It's our job to take apart each of these similar Answer Choices and find that difference wherever it may be (in the (5), (10), (15) or even (20)).

iii) after you've found the difference between the Answer Choices, you select the Answer Choice with the more stand-out information in it *i.e.* the Brad Pitt.

If, after attempting your Marking Map, the Answer Choices have a strange combination of results (no clear answer), you're being sent a signal that your Essence is incorrect. Now you:

i) refer back to the Text and try to find the correct Essence. If you still have no luck then return to the Answer Choices and...

ii) use the Hierarchy of Importance and Bottom-Line to eliminate surplus details in the Answer Choice so you can find the core of each Answer Choices. This will force you to focus on what's most important and ignore distracting details within the Answer *Choices*.

Two correct answers?

In some cases, you might complete your Marking Map and find (omg!) two answers are 100% correct. Could ETS have made an error in the exam? Nope! Let's consider an example:

"While other employees were learning that in Australia you get what you demand, I was being dictated to my office supplies. While other employees were learning to find their own voices, I was struggling to control my business attire, my office PC and my stationery."

Q: The writer of this paragraph implies he felt different from other employees because?

(A) they hardly faced the turmoil he had to face daily.

(B) he was encouraged to assert himself.

(C) his boss enjoyed criticizing his poor work ethic.

(D) he was not able to express himself.

(E) he didn't know how to take care of his work equipment compared to other employees.

I've had students swear to me that both (A) and (D) are correct – "no doubt about it!" What's weird here is that we can easily see that these Answer Choices are totally different. In most of our previous examples, we focused on matching problems that were the result of Answer Choices that appeared similar.

So what's going on?

Both answers *do* supply us with factually correct information but the problem is (again) we have the wrong Essence. Students who believed (A) to be correct are constructing their Essence, using irrelevant information – they're not focusing on the central point of the paragraph. This is why these students are having difficulty with eliminating.

When you're tackling questions, make sure the Essence you find matches with what the question is actually asking for! To see what I've described, look at the following Table.

Answer Choice Table with the Complete Essence:

	Essence	(A)	(D)
5	Man	They	Man
10	—	—	—
15	Personal Difficulties	Turmoil	Felt limited
20		"he had to face daily"	

The Essence of this entire paragraph is "a man having personal difficulties." The only Answer choice that matches with this Essence is (D). Why not (A)?

First, the topic (5) of this Answer Choice is incorrect. The Essence calls for a topic focused on "the man," not on "they" (you can see I've X'ed the boxes that don't match our Essence – I'll be doing a lot more of this in our review of Test 1 in the Appendix).

Secondly, the theme (15) of this Answer Choice (turmoil) is a stylistically awkward word choice even if it seems close to the Essence theme of "difficulty." Finally, the inclusion of the details (20) – "*he had to face daily*" – in the Answer Choice should give us pause because there wasn't this kind of specific information in the Text.

Remember: 'Brad Pitt' is very specific information in the Answer Choice that you can compare with the Text. So we have an incorrect, overly specific Answer Choice that has no objective support from the Text!

Let's look at an example of this – <u>Page 83 #24</u>. Please try and answer the question for yourself before you move on.

Answer Choices (B) and (E) are completely out of the range of possible answers. However, if you landed on (A), (C), and (D), I can sympathize and I'll break down where your confusion is coming from!

To begin our analysis, let's examine a Table for these three most prominent Answer Choices.

<u>Answer Choice Table with the Essence:</u>

	Essence	(A)	(C)	(D)
5	Parents	Their Departure	Decision	Departure
10	–	–	N	–
15	Acknowledge pain	Recognize distress	Ambivalent	Pain
20	"much as they wanted it"		Great deal	So great

<u>Scenario 1:</u>

In this scenario, let's say you're confused between (A) and (D). You've successfully tabled both of these Answer Choices, but the difference at the (5), (10), and (15) level is too slight for you to distinguish. Fortunately, (D) contains the Brad Pitt phrase "so great" (similar to "*he had to face daily*" in the previous example). Can we link this with anything in the text? No! (D) is our *incorrect* answer and (A) is our winner!

<u>Scenario 2:</u>

In this scenario, suppose you're stuck between (A) and (C). The reason for this is probably because you've picked up "much as they wanted it" (line 69) and thought something like, "ah so there is pain and desire, so this is a good match with (C) ambivalence."

However, if you read critically, you'll see this was just included to add to the central point that the parents were feeling pain. These *details* are not the central point, but rather just support it. So (A) is correct because it matches with the Essence of "pain." This example again demonstrates how critical it is not to get lost in the irrelevant details when you are constructing your Essence.

138 James Hong

The Characteristics of Incorrect Answer Choices

Well done! You've covered a lot of important ground in this chapter. The final thing you're going to learn here is short and sweet: the characteristics of incorrect Answer Choices.

Unmentioned Info: The Answer Choice contains information that wasn't mentioned anywhere in the Text. This is usually the easiest error to find in the First Round but there are cases when it's subtle and usually Brad Pitt is the technique of choice.

False: Information in the Answer Choice is indeed mentioned in the Text but this information contradicts what was actually said within the Text. These are slightly more difficult than unmentioned information questions. The approach of choice here is to view this as a Double-Column question and carefully examine the Answer Choices using Top-Down and Brad-Pitt.

Irrelevant Information: The Answer Choice contains information that isn't relevant to what the question is asking (as in the "much as they wanted it" example we just covered). Your best bet here is to make these Answer Choices Single-Column (through Bottom-Line) and examine them using the Hierarchy of Information.

Stylistically awkward: The Answer Choice is written in a clumsy way. For example, the Answer Choice may contain words that are too strong for a situation ("turmoil" instead of "difficulty"). When you judge an Answer Choice as Stylistically Awkward you need to be careful because this is still a subjective judgment after all. For this reason, it's not recommended you solely eliminate an Answer Choice based on something awkward. However, if the other typical incorrect Answer Choice characteristics don't reveal themselves, use this as your final elimination tool.

That's it! Keep these categories in mind as you begin to attempt various Answer Choices.

We've covered a lot of ground here so I'm pretty sure a number of you are still a little confused. Not a problem! To remedy this, please visit us online for a collection of problem sets that focus on things like Theme Matching, Counterbalancing and Brad Pitt, and a lot more!

Congratulations!
Now you've got SAT CR at your finger tips!

POST GAME RECAP

We're at the end of our Gaming strategy session!

Let's look back at what we've learned.

I started off with Macro Management which introduced you to the concept of having a solid base for attacking the test. This base was created through effectively managing your time and sorting questions correctly.

Our journey then led us to look at what exactly it means to be a critical reader for the SAT. We focused on the importance of reading objectively and how to extract meaning from vocabulary, sentences, paragraphs, and passages.

Next, we steered toward analyzing each of the elements that are included in the SAT Critical Reading section – the Questions, Text, Essence, and Answer Choices. My analysis here was split between the Opening (where I categorized Questions and found ways to search for the Essence within the Text) and the Closing (where you learned how to eliminate incorrect Answer Choices and select correct Answer Choices).

I hope you enjoyed this journey as much as I enjoyed writing about it! Now before you plunge into the solutions to Test 1, I'd like to take a few minutes to chat to you about a few other things.

Where to from here?

First, in my experience, what you've just learned cannot be *fully* understood and applied after just one reading. It usually takes students two or three reviews of the material before they finally put all the pieces together. So please, don't just give it a once-over and then move on – go back and read it once or twice more if necessary. Don't prematurely attempt further tests in the Blue Book before you know and understand the concepts I have discussed. The Blue Book tests exist to help you figure out whether you can effectively apply what you have learned to actual ETS material.

Have patience in trying the techniques you've learned and give them time to settle. How are you going to take what you know and make it second nature? Through a lot of practice! A single test won't be enough to master this material. For best results, finish the rest of the tests in the Blue Book.

If you're looking for even more resources to practice with, visit www.CollegeBoard.org and download this year's "The SAT Preparation Booklet" (to find copies from prior years just search Google). In this booklet, you'll find a real SAT exam that's previously been administered. I'll be releasing resources to help you with the exams in these booklets soon!

Second, vocabulary is another area I've really emphasized throughout the books, and without wanting to nag, I really can't stress enough how important it is for you to work on your vocabulary. This is particularly true for lower level students. Without a reasonable level of vocabulary proficiency, your prospects of SAT success are uncertain. Make it your goal to go out and study just a few words each and every day!

Finally, remember the SAT is just a game. Yes, everyone goes on and on about how important it is but this is not the way I want you to think about it. To you, it's a Game you enjoy playing and that's all. You are *bigger* than the SAT since you are the player. You control it rather than it controls you. Keep this commanding, but lighthearted attitude toward the test. If you do badly while practicing, so what? You can always insert more quarters and restart the Game as many times as you want!

Are you ready? Then go out and get Gaming and Winning!

APPENDIX

Solutions to Test 1

This is the practical part of the book where you'll see the various tools, techniques and strategies you've learned being applied to actual SAT questions.

Some notes before we move on to the questions:

Notation:

- **O**: an element that *could* be correct
- Δ: an element that many students believe to be correct but actually isn't
- **?**: an element that many students don't know
- **Diagonal Line through box/X:** an element that doesn't match with the Essence

Approach:

- Although I've given you the Cherry for most questions, I'd like you to try and find it for yourself first. In some cases, there is a brief explanation about the Cherry. I've also noted any important Flag-Words for select SentCom question.
- A Top-Down style Table for most questions has been added including topic (5), evaluation (10), theme (15), and details (20) of the Essence and each Answer Choice.
- When a question illustrates an important concept, there is a brief discussion.
- When there is important vocabulary to learn, I've added some tricks to help you.

Are you ready? Then let's dive in!

\<Section 2\>

Question 1: (A)

<u>Cherry</u>: "Predict"

<u>Flag-Word</u>: "when" – we're looking for a theme match.

	Essence	(A)	(B)	(C)	(D)	(E)
5	Adjective	O		O	O	O
10	+	+	N	~	~	+
15	Predict	Foresee	Old times	Silly	Sadness	Skillful

At the topic (5) level, I use OXΔ as a measure of how well an Answer Choice seems to subjectively fit a blank – just go with your ears here, there is no magic formula. Answer Choice (B) "nostalgia," for example, just seems odd and a bad fit, so I mark it X.

If you missed the Cherry in the First Round, you could still use this Top-Down Table to eliminate Answer Choices that don't match with the Essence. Only (A) perfectly aligns with the Essence.

Question 2: (B)

<u>Cherry</u>: "Simple," "Direct"

<u>Flag-Word</u>: "reflection" – we're looking for a theme match.

<u>Explanation</u>: Theme matching "candid" means white (think of a candle); honest, pure (a candidate is a person who needs to be honest).

	Essence	(A)	(B)	(C)	(D)	(E)
5	Reflection		O	Δ	O	O
10	+	N	+			
15	Simple, Direct	Complex	Forthright	Showy	Unreal	Complicated

Vocabulary: \

convoluted – "con" (together - *e.g.* conspire, contract, condone) , "vol" (turning – *e.g.* revolving). So everything is moving together and confused.

ostentatious – think of Austen (pronounced the same, as in OSTENtatious) Powers, very showy and over the top!☺

Question 3: (A)

Cherry: "Impulsive," "Whim"

Flag-Words: "led," "label" – cause and effect theme matching.

	Essence	(A)	(B)	(C)	(D)	(E)
5	Nature	O	O	O	O	Δ
10	–	–	–	–	N	+
15	Impulsive, sudden whim	Unstable	Arrogant Δ/?	Talkative	Composure	Well mannered

Vocabulary:

Loquacious – "loq" (relates to talking – eloquent, colloquial etc) this is talking too much.

Decorous – "decorate" (cover yourself in a graceful air).

Question 4: (D)

Cherry: "visceral," "rational"

Flag-Words: "rather than," "not so much…as" – opposite theme matching *i.e.* negation.

	Essence		(C)		(D)		(E)	
5	Judgment	O	O	O	O	O	O
10	N	–	+	–	N	–	N	+
15	Mental process	Intuition	Instinct Δ/?	Quickly Δ	Planned	Hunch	Purpose Δ	Logic

Question 5: (C)

Cherry: "versatility," "adaptability," "rigid"

Flag-Word: "as a result of" – cause and effect.

Explanation: "Ossify" shares themes with *fossilized*, petrified etc. all related to stones (image of rigidity), "bureaucracy" has a similar theme (slow moving – think of any government agency). "Versatility" has a theme of wide range or adaptability (think of "*reverse*" or "*conversant*") that relates to turning, movement or reach.

	Essence		(A)		(B)		(D)		(E)	
5	Creative Stratagem	O	O		O	O	O			O
10	–	–	+	–	+	–	–	+	+	N
15	Rigid	Rigid	simple △	fight	Lessen	bias △	Political	New	Respect	Law

The last question in SentCom usually has very tricky vocabulary in it. If you're a low scoring student, you should probably just skip this question (be mindful of your Macro-Management) and move on to other questions where you can more efficiently use your time.

If you're still facing a mountain of unknown words in this question remove all simple vocabulary words from consideration. So we'd eliminate (A) "infighting," (D) "innovation," and (E) "legislation." Now we're left with (B) "mitigated…jingoism" and (C) "ossified… bureaucracy" – the difficult and correct answer.

Vocabulary:

Streamlined – "Stream" (movement like a stream) flowing constantly from point A to point B *i.e.* highly efficient.

Questions 6-7 are based on the following Passage

Why	Describe
5	Being a Human
10	+
15	Goodness

Question 6: (D)

Cherry: "Wondrous spectacle" (line 10)

Flag-Word: "They never" – contrast

Explanation: The theme is, "wonder is amazing," so you appreciate things that make you feel amazed (unlike the wild-horses).

	Essence	(A)	(B)	(C)	(E)
5	Nature		People	Past △	Joy △
10	+		+	N	+
15	Wondrous	Mistake	Companionship	Reflect △	Seeking
20					Simple

Question 7: (B)

Cherry: "Whistling and moaning"(line 1), "river of clouds"(line 3), "punishing wind"(line 6) etc.

Explanation: The above examples are metaphors.

	Essence	(A)	(C)	(D)	(E)
Why	Metaphor	Pathos	Analogy	Memories	Irony

Rhetorical Devices: Refer to Appendix for more other rhetorical devices.

Questions 8-9 are based on the following Passage

Why	Sum up
5	Ada King
10	+
15	Fame

Question 8: (C)

Cherry: No Cherry since this is a general question. Refer to the above Table.

Explanation: The theme (15) of the Passage is "fame" which theme matches with "celebrated."

	Essence	(A)	(B)	(C)	(D)	(E)
Why	Sum up	Explain	analysis	Summary	Trace	Encourage
5	Ada King	Ada King	Ada King	Ada King	Computer	Women's careers in CS
10	+	N	N	+	N	N
15	Fame	CS interest △		Celebrated	Development	Pursue

Answer Choice (A) shows how surplus details put into an Answer Choice can be misleading – the (20) of "interest in Computer Science" is not the primary concern of the Passage (irrelevant info as in characteristics of wrong answer choices).

Question 9: (A)

Cherry: "Lineage" (line 7)

Explanation: "Lineage" finds its theme match with "Family."

	Essence	(A)	(B)	(C)	(D)	(E)
5	Life, lineage	Family history	Contribution	Interest	Her fame in CS	Her life
10	+	–	+	+	+	+
15	Famous	No part	Original	Spread	famous	Remarkable
20	Lord Byron		Markedly	Popular culture	Completed her work	Contribution to CS

This question is a bit different because here we're asked to look for a sentence that the author would *disagree* with. Don't be tempted to look at the Answer Choices before you formulate an Essence!

The thesis of this Passage is King's "fascinating life and lineage." Using this, we can eliminate (B), (C), and (D) because they focus on incidental details and not the big picture. Our final battle is between (A) and (E) and since we're looking for something incorrect, we can safely eliminate (E) because we know that King did many things in addition to her contribution to Computer Science.

This leaves (A) as our answer.

Questions10-15 are based on the following Passage

Why	Emphasize
5	Relationship between African-Americans and Africans
10	+
15	Important

Question 10: (D)

Cherry: No Cherry since this is a general question. Refer to the above Table.

Explanation: "Strong" ties important theme matches with "significance of ongoing relationship."

	Essence	(A)	(B)	(C)	(D)	(E)
Why	Emphasize	Show	Discuss	Point out	Emphasize	Examine △
5	Tie between African-Americans and Africans	Black Americans and African societies △	Africans vs. American Culture	Between communities △	Ongoing relationship	two nations
10	+	N	+	N	+	N
15	Important	Impact △	Embrace	Ambivalence	Important	Cultural ties

Question 11: (B)

Cherry: "adage" (line 5)

Explanation: this Answer Choice is the very definition of an adage.

	Essence	(A)	(B)	(C)	(D)	(E)
10	+	−	+	−	N	+
15	Adage	Criticism	Advice	Proposition	Recollection	Prediction
20		Veiled	Cautionary ?	Questionable	Nostalgic	Optimistic

Question 12: (C)

Cherry: "pull of one's heritage…" (line 17)

Explanation: "History" theme matches with "heritage."

	Essence	(A)	(B)	(C)	(D)	(E)
Why	Indicate	Offer	Emphasize	Show	Demonstrate	Warn
5	People	Children's behavior	Children	People	Familial relations △	People vs. Family △
10	+	+		+		
15	Heritage	Insight	Vulnerable	history	Complex	Undermine
20		Young		inherent		Family

Question 13: (E)

Cherry: "imaginings"(line 41), "real" (line 42)

Explanation: "Real experience" is unlike "shadowy imaginings" *i.e.* unsubstantiated.

	Essence	(A)	(B)	(C)	(D)	(E)
5	Imagining	△	△	△		O
10	−	−	− /N △	−	−	−
15	Nebulous	Dark	Hidden △	Bad	Hidden △	Unproven

In this question, you'd probably have difficulty with (B) "secret" or (D) "concealed" and (E) "unsubstantiated." Bottom-Line each Answer-Choice (our result is hidden v. unproven). From structurally analyzing the sentence, we have an Essence of "Unreal" or "Nebulous." Is "hidden" truly the opposite of "real" ? Nope. (E) is our answer.

Question 14: (E)

Cherry: "wonder"(line 43), "world take note…"(line 50)

Flag-Word: "but" – reversal

Explanation: "wonder" (uncertainty) i.e. doubt; "world take note "(centre stage) i.e. pride.

	Essence		(C)		(E)	
5	Feelings					
10	–	+	–		–	+
15	Wonder	Take note	Uncertainty	Despair	Doubt	Pride

Question 15: (B)

Cherry: Last sentence, "And when we…forced to take note."(line 47)

Explanation: Since the question asks for the author's overall device to convey his point, your best bet is in the last sentence where he speaks in general. Here the author uses "we…we.." – a clear indication of generalization.

	(A)	(B)	(C)	(D)	(E)
5	Scenario	Generalization	Facts △	Anecdotes	Analyses △
10	N	N	N	N	N
20	Hypothetical	Broad	Historical △	Personal	Scholarly

Vocabulary:

Scenario – a hypothetical situation
Anecdote – a personal story
Scholarly – written in a balanced and measured way

Questions 16-24 are based on the following Passages

	Passage 1	Passage 2
Why	Emphasize	Explanation
5	Mona Lisa's Fame	Mona Lisa's Fame
10	N	N
15	Good technique	Diverse conditions leading to fame

Question 16: (C)

<u>Cherry</u>: No Cherry since this is a general question. Refer to the above Table.

<u>Explanation</u>: "fame" theme matches with "popular appeal."

	Essence	(A)	(B)	(D)	(E)
5	Mona Lisa	Smile	Identity	Artist	Condition
10	+	+	N	+	—
15	Fame	Mysterious		Influence	Deteriorating

Question 17: (A)

<u>Cherry</u>: No Cherry. It asks for the main theme of Passage 2. Refer to the above Table for Passage 2.

<u>Explanation</u>: Our theme of Passage 2 is "diverse conditions leading to fame" which theme matches with "a sequence of event…for different ends." (lines 68-70)

	(A)	(B)	(C)	(D)	(E)
5	Circumstances	Occurrences $\triangle$	Art enthusiasts	Events	Facts
10	N	—	—	—	—
15	Contributed to fame	Distort the importance	Annoyed	Unworthy	Inconvenient
20	Themselves	Fundamentally, true	Unduly	Art critic's consideration	Many art historians

Question 18: (E)

Cherry: "nobody special" (line 7) and "But set the standard for…many important ways." (line 8)

Explanation: "nobody special" theme matches with "ordinary"; "important" theme matches with "significant."

	(A)		(B)		(C)		(D)	
5	Appearance	Beauty Δ	Origins	Value	Demise	Immortality	Charisma	Allure
10	−	+	−	N	−	+	−	+
20	unremarkable	Astonishing	Humble	Money	Untimely		Lack of	Universal

Question 19: (B)

Cherry: "this techniques renders (produces) the whole" (line 23)

Explanation: product: effect; to define: to characterize

	Essence	(A)	(B)	(C)	(D)	(E)
Why	Define	Defend	Characterize	Criticize	Downplay	Acknowledge
5	product	Methodology Δ	Effect	Technique Δ	Accomplishment Δ	Influence
10	N	+	N	−	−	N

Question 20: (A)

Cherry: "that famous smile" (line 29)

Explanation: "smile" matches with "mouth."

Question 21: (D)

Cherry: "idea" (line 40)

Explanation: "idea" theme matches with "view."

	Essence	(A)	(B)	(C)	(E)
5	Art critics			△	
10	N	N	N	N	N
15	Idea	Class	Position	Rules	Place

Remember: put words in the context and watch out for the "everyday" meaning of words.

Question 22: (E)

Cherry: Passage 2 "Sense of texture and depth" (line 56), "three dimensional effect" (lines 21-22)

	Essence	(A)	(B)	(C)
5	Technique	Viewers	General Public	Generations of artists
10	+	+	-	+
15	3D	Respond	Revere	Influence
20		Idiosyncratic	Unduly	Many

Question 23: (E)

Cherry: "avoid succumbing…myth" (lines 59-60)

Explanation: Self-explanatory

	Essence	(A)	(B)	(C)	(D)	(E)
Why	Disagree	Label	Refer to	Emphasize	Highlight	Imply
5	Idea	Movement	Art technique	Term △	Finding △	Theory
10	−	+	−	N	+	−
15	Dubious	Revolutionary	Overused	Symbolic	Importance	Skeptical

Question 24: (C)

<u>Cherry</u>: Refer back to the Passage Table theme (15)

<u>Explanation</u>: "Good technique" theme matches with "stylistic innovation," "fame" theme matches with "cultural preeminence."

<Section 5>

Question 1: (C)

<u>Cherry</u>: "Eagerly welcomes"

<u>Explanation</u>: "Welcome" theme matches with "hospitality."

Question 2: (B)

<u>Cherry</u>: "Disappointed," "supporters"

<u>Flag-Words</u>: "Not surprisingly," "when"

<u>Explanation</u> : Supporters of something would be disappointed if something was rejected.

	Essence	(A)	(B)	(C)	(D)	(E)
5	Decision		O	O	O	△
10	−	+	−	N	+	+
15	Rejected	Praise	Stop	Admit	Allow	Predict

Question 3: (C)

Cherry: "Increase," "promote"

Flag-Words: "Because," "[in order] to"

Explanation: theme matching with "increase"/"promote"

	Essence	(C)	(D)	(E)
5	Musical instrument	O		
10	+	+	N	+
15	Increase promote	Increase	Noteworthy	Rest

Question 4: (A)

Cherry: "subtle…difference"

Flag-Word: "but"

Explanation: a marginal antonym match

	Essence		(B)	(C)		(D)		(E)	
5	Country		O	O	O	O		O	
10	N	N	+				N		
15	Difference	Fight	Ally	Give up	Enemy	Control	Ask	Doubt	Curse

If you simplify, you should be able to tell the antonym theme between "negotiate" – to strive to work out – and "concessions" – to accept with a negotiation .

Vocabulary:

Respite – "re" (again), "spite" (spirit) so it means to renew or refresh through rest.

Question 5: (D)

<u>Cherry</u>: "taken from another artist," "poorly executed"

<u>Explanation</u>: simply theme match Cherries with Answer Choice

	(A)		(B)		(C)		(E)	
5	O	O	O	△	O	O		
10	+	+	–	N	–	+	N	–
15	Awake	Memory	Boring	Changing	Confusion	New	Instant	No style △

<u>Vocabulary</u>:

Inept – "In" means "not," "apt" means "fit," so unfit i.e. not good.

Pedestrian – "Ped" relates to legs and feet (e.g. pedal). Think of regular, average pedestrians just walking on the street. Boring! Keep that image of 'average' in your mind because that's just what "pedestrian" means in this situation – average, not special, not eye catching.

Equivocate – "equi" (equal) and "voca" (with voice as in "vocabulary," "vocalist") so you have many voices and hence there is confusion and no result. "Equivocate" means you use unclear expressions.

Unprecedented – "Un" (never), "pre" (before), "cede" (go- e.g. "recede," "concede") i.e. something that's never happened before.

Question 6: (B)

Flag-Word: "by making" – cause and effect

	Essence	(A)		(C)		(D)		(E)	
5	Method vs. industry		△	O	△			O	O
10	+	+		+	+			+	
15	Inexpensive, nascent	Poor △	Cheap △	New	Stop	Excite	Slim	Excite	Not open
20	Commercially								

(A) is incorrect because "cheapened" does not mean "cheap" it means of a low quality.

Question 7: (D)

Cherry: "haughty"

Explanation: theme match "haughty" with "supercilious"

	Text	Essence	(A)	(B)	(C)	(E)
5	Philip	Manner	O	O		△
10	–	–	–	+	+	–
15	Haughty	Haughty, winning	Secret	Wise	Joy	Fight
20	After winning, treating friends					

Vocabulary:

pugnacious – "pugn" (fight: e.g. "impugn," "repugnant") all share the same theme.

Supercilious – "super" meaning over the top, to the extreme, "cili" means "eyelid" so it means your eyelids top other people's i.e. being arrogant and looking down on others.

Judicious: being a good "judge."

Question 8: (C)

Cherry: "Disloyalty"

Flag-Words: "suspected," "synonymous"

	Essence	(A)	(B)	(D)	(E)
5	The general	O	△		O
10	–	–	–	–	+
15	Disloyalty	Fight	Poor	Dislike	Endurance
20	Suspected, Synonymous				

Vocabulary:

Belligerent – "bell" (war or battle: e.g. "bellicose"). Think of a beautiful woman with the name of "IsaBELLa" whom many men want to fight over.

Perfidy – "fid" (loyalty and trust as in "*fid*elity," "conf*id*e," or "*fid*uciary"). Here "per" means opposite, so "perfidy" means breaking a trust (disloyalty).

Note: the most common meaning of "*per*" is "thoroughness" ("perfect," "pervade," "pertain") however.

Question 9-12 are based on the following Passages

	Passage 1		Passage 2	
Why	Explain		Argue	
5	Thoreau v. nature		Thoreau v. mechanization	
10	N	N	N	+
15	Worship		Productive garden	

Question 9: (A)

Cherry: the above Table while for the teachers in Passage 1, it is "anti-industrialization."

	Teachers		Passage 2	
5	Nature threatened		Thoreau v mechanization	
10	–	–	N	+
15	Protest		Productive garden	

The Table shows that the teachers are focused on the idea that Thoreau was negative about industrialization. The author of Passage 2 on the other hand, believes Thoreau had a more positive perspective.

	Essence	(A)	(B)	(C)	(D)	(E)
5	Nature vs. machine	Nature	Thoreau's experiment	Walden as a work of literature	urbanization	Walden's topic
10	–	–	+	+	N	+
15	Intrusion	Threatened	Recounted	Important	Spread △	Power of the machine △

Question 10: (B)

Cherry: "intrusion into pastoral harmony"

Explanation: theme match the Cherry with "…destructive of nature's tranquility"

	Essence	(A)	(B)	(C)	(D)	(E)
5	Nature	Nature	Nature	people	Nature	Nature
10	–	N	–	–	+	N
15	Intrusion into	Stopped △	Destructive	Exaggerated	Necessary	Less threatening △
20		Comparable	Tranquility	Not seeking out nature	Productive	Living close to

Question 11: (E)

Cherry: "downright enthusiastic"

Flag-Words: "although," "at other times"

	Passage 1		Passage 2	
5	Thoreau v. nature		Thoreau v. mechanization	
10	N	N	N	+
15	Worship		Enthusiastic	

	Essence	(A)	(B)	(C)	(D)
5	Thoreau	Walden v. industrialization	Response	Teachers v. Thoreau's character	Thoreau's experiment v. His attitude
10	+		N	N	N
15	Worship nature	Regret	Resonated with	Emphasized	Derived
20			19th century Americans		Solitary living

Keep this question simple (in fact you don't even need the second table). How does passage 1's author view Thoreau? As a nature lover. How is Thoreau cast in line 14? As a lover of industrialization.

We're looking at line 14 from the perspective of the author of Passage 2. How do you think he'd react if someone said Thoreau was a big fan of industrialization? He'd probably be extremely shocked and think this was totally untrue i.e. "atypical."

Question 12: (C)

Cherry: "as an illustration… the intrusion" (line 7), "he was downright enthusiastic" (line 3)

	Essence	(A)	(B)	(D)	(E)
5	Nature v. Walden	Machine	American v. nature	Railroad v. Thoreau's enthusiasm	Thoreau's time v now
10	+	–	–	–	+
15	Worship	Destructive	Influence	Overlook	In accord with
20	Anti-industrialization		Long-standing		

Question 13-24 are based on the following Passage

5	Cities	
10	N	+
15	Natural	

Question 13: (D)

Cherry: "Notion" (line 13)

	Essence	(A)	(B)	(C)	(E)
5	City	O	O	Δ	
10	N	N		N	
15	Opinion	Unrealistic	Lie	Prediction	Unclear

Question 14: (D)

Cherry: "hackles up," (line 2) "unnatural" (line 3)

	Passage 1		Line 9	
5	Cities		Cities	
10	N	+	−	−
15	Natural		Unnatural	

The Cherries signal the author's opinion on the "happier state." The fact that quotation marks are used here shows the authors cynicism for this description. When you consider these quotation marks and the words "gets my hackles up" (to get angry or irritated about something) you can see the author considers the idea that cities are somehow unnatural as ridiculous.

	Essence	(A)	(B)	(C)	(E)
5	Idea	Solution	Luck	Arrangement	Memory
10	−	+	+	−	−
15	Wrong	Satisfactory		Complicated	Bittersweet

Vocabulary:

Supposition - "suppose" (think, consider), "sup[b]" (under, underlying *e.g.* "supplementary," "subway"), "pose" (take a position).

Question 15: (E)

Cherry: "a wrong turning" (line 20)

	Essence	(A)	(B)	(C)	(D)	(E)
5	Trend	Example	Instance	Era △	Time △	Trend
10	−	+	N	+	N	−
15	Wrong turn	Important human achievement	Double edged potential △	Self sufficient	Transcend the distinction	Harmful

Question 16: (E)

Cherry: "bothers" (line 26)

	Passage 1		thinkers
5	Cities		Nature
10	N	+	N
15	Natural		No people
20			Cities stop nature

	Essence	(A)	(B)	(C)	(D)	(E)
5	Thinkers views					
10	–	+	+	–	–	–
15	Wrong	Reasoning	Though provoking	Unintelligible	Inconclusive	Erroneous
20		Carefully				

Question 17: (B)

Cherry: "they aren't unnatural" (line 33)

	Essence	(A)	(B)	(C)	(D)	(E)
Why	Give example	Explain	Suggest	Assert	Point out	Call attention to
5	Beaver Dams and Anthills	Ecological systems △	Products	All three	Different species	Obstacles
10	N	N	N	–	N	–
15	Natural products	Work	Natural impulses	Detrimental	Flourish	
20				Ultimately	Different environments	Facing cities today

Question 18: (E)

<u>Cherry</u>: "all of…food sources" (line 52)

	Essence	(A)	(B)	(C)	(D)	(E)
10	+			N		+
15	Acknowledgment	Sad	Irritation	Neutral	Carefree	Appreciation

Question 19: (A)

<u>Cherry</u>: "at least" (line 58)

	Essence	(A)	(B)	(C)	(D)	(E)
Why	Explore	Present	Organize	Illustrate	Group	Compare
5	Opinions	Arguments	opinion △	Assertion and conclusion	Hypothesis	Theories △
10	N	N	N	N	N	
15	Supporting	support	most to least Important	initial to ultimate	Opposing	Alternative
20		Fundamental		Reasoning		Scientific community

Question 20: (D)

<u>Cherry</u>: "peculiar"

	Essence	(A)	(B)	(C)	(D)	(E)
5	Collection	△	O	O	O	△
10	+	N		N	+	+
15	Peculiar	Strange	Weird	Unusual	Unique	Important
20	Flora and fauna					

Question 21: (A)

Cherry: "accolade" (line 65)

	Essence	(A)	(B)
5			
10	+	+	+
15	Accolade	Approval	Curiosity
20			

Question 22: (C)

Cherry: "both…both" (lines 69-73)

	(A)	(B)	(C)	(D)	(E)
Definition	Attempted justification	Granting	Comparing	Excluded from a general statement	Implication
What would be in the text	"The point I'm making is valid due to the following reasons…"	"Granted, I could have made a mistake with collecting the data but…"	"Both were handsome, both were intelligent and both worked hard…"	"Generally, students work hard but there are a few atypical students who choose not to…"	"It seems like it's rained for 40 days and nights…" (this is a reference to Noah's Arc)

On this table, I've taken a slightly different approach. Instead of analyzing each of the Answer Choices, I've given a definition of each characterization and then an example of how it might appear in the Text.

Question 23: (E)

Cherry: "well defined rules of nature" (line 75)

	Essence	(A)	(B)	(C)	(D)	(E)
5	Law of nature v. cities	Cities △	Cities △	Cities △	Human efforts △	Natural principles v Human endeavors
10	N	+	–	N		N
15	Limitation	Ability to change and grow	Larger	Self regulating	Backfire	Affect
20			Than they need to be	to survive	To conquer nature	Significantly

Question 24: (E)

Cherry: "So let me state this explicitly:"(line 82)

	Essence	(A)	(B)	(C)	(D)	(E)
Why	Emphasize	Restate △	Summarize △	Heighten	Suggest	Emphasize
5	Author's idea	Dilemma	Authors advice	Impact	Focus for Research	Author's position
10	N	N	N	+	N	N
15						
20				Emotional	Further	

<Section 9>

Question 1: (B)

<u>Cherry</u>: "stylistic tricks or evasiveness"

<u>Flag-Word</u>: "free of"

	Essence	(A)	(B)	(C)	(D)	(E)
5	Prose	O	O	O	Δ	Δ
10	+		+			
15	Stylistic tricks or evasiveness	Inexact	Direct	Lacking	Disruptive	Unclear
20	Free					

<u>Vocabulary</u>:

Obtrusive – "ob" (against – think objection) "trude" (sticking out, interfering – intruder, protrude etc)

Question 2: (C)

<u>Cherry</u>: "size of the crowd," "resonance of its cheers"

<u>Flag-Words</u>: "which was," "which were" (apposition/synonym)

	(A)		(B)		(C)		(D)		(E)	
5	O	Δ	O	O	O	O	O	Δ	O	O
10	+			+	+	+/–				+
15	Big	Empty	Few	Loud	Big	Loud	Normal	Silent	Little	Uplifting Δ

Question 3: (B)

<u>Flag-Word</u>: "thus caused" – cause and effect (synonym)

	(A)		(B)		(C)		(D)		(E)	
5	O	Δ	O	O	O	Δ	Δ	O	Δ	Δ
10	+	–	N	N	–	+	+	–	–	+
15	Forward	Backward	Change	Change	Reverse	Pause	Emphasize	Danger	Stop	Breach

Question 4: (E)

<u>Cherry</u>: Gained (indicates a positive evaluation).

<u>Flag-Words</u>: "although," "still"

	(A)		(B)		(C)		(D)		(E)	
5	O	O		O	O	O	O		O	O
10	+	+	–	–	+	+	+	N	+	–
15	Trust	Undeniable	Poor reputation	Doubt	Admit	Sure	Speed	Organized	Trend	Unstable

Question 5: (B)

<u>Cherry</u>: "transparent"

<u>Flag-Word</u>: "so…as to be"

	Essence	(A)	(C)	(D)	(E)
5	Fabrics	Δ	O	O	Δ
10	N	N	N	+	N
15	Transparent	Conerete	Diverse	Expensive	Strange
20	So…as to				

<u>Vocabulary</u> :

Diaphanous – "di" (double, two of e.g. "dissect," "dialect," "dichotomous"), "phan" (can't be seen, think "phantom"). So here, think of two phantoms (ghosts) which are virtually transparent (not completely transparent, but with some form) on top of each other.

Luxurious – "lux" (comes from light, shining think of gold e.g. "lucrative," "translucent," "lucid")

Variegated – think "variety" (many types of)

Anomalous – think "anomaly" (one of).

Question 6: (D)

<u>Cherry</u>: "attacked cherished beliefs"

<u>Flag-Word</u>: "as" – synonym

	Essence	(A)	(B)	(C)	(E)
5	Reputation	O	O	O	
10	– or N	+	N	–	N
15	Disdain tradition, attacked cherished beliefs	Equal	Old woman	Amateur	Giver

<u>Vocabulary</u> :

Iconoclast – "icon" + "clash" – someone who goes against established traditions or orthodoxies.

Purveyor – "veyor" (carries something *e.g.* conveyor belt)

<u>Questions 7-19 are based on the following Passage</u>

5	Miss Keeldar and Mr. Sympson (Uncle)	
10	N	–
15	Arguing about marriage partner	

Question 7: (C)

Cherry: No Cherry since this is a general question. Refer to the Table in the previous page.

	Essence	(A)	(B)	(C)	(D)	(E)
5	Keeldar & Mr. Sympson	Family relationship	Woman △	People	Two individuals	Extended family
10	N	–	–	–	–	+	+
15	Arguing about marriage partner	Setback △	Disappointment	Confrontation	Collaboration	Conversation
20	Keeldar and Mr. Sympson (Uncle)	Otherwise warm	Young and ambitious △	Irreconcilable	Similar goal	Unity

Question 8: (C)

Cherry: "spirited," (line 3) "freedom" (line 4) versus "despotic," (line 3) "worldly" (line 4)

Flag-Word: "would not harmonize" (line 2) – contrasting parallelism

	Essence	(A)	(B)	(C)	(D)	(E)
5	Lifestyle	Others	Good husband	Ideas about life	Books and poetry about love	Subject of stories
10	+	+	–	+	N	–
15	Spirited, freedom	Attractive and mysterious	Concerned with finding	Passionate and unconventional	Prefers to read	Is
20		Seems	Overly			Fancifully exaggerated

Question 9: (E)

<u>Cherry</u>: "he intended to discharge it," (line 7) "wash…forever" (line 10)

<u>Flag-Word</u>: "his mission" (line 7)

	Essence	(A)	(B)	(C)	(D)	(E)
5	Family responsibility	Project	Nieces goal	Families reputation △	Opportunity to his niece	Family responsibility
10	–	N	+	–	–	–
15	Get rid of	Anticipation	Eager to help realize	Apprehension	Frustration	Impatience to free himself
20	"consciously and anxiously"	Collaboration	Ambitious	Tarnished	Limited	Perceived

Don't forget the importance of beacons. In this question, the beacon is "motivated by" which dovetails well with "his mission" (line 7) so we know the Cherry (line 7, 10) will be shortly after this.

Question 10: (E)

<u>Cherry</u>: "A fine…connections" (line 22)

<u>Flag-Word</u>: "decidedly suitable" (line 20)

	Essence	(A)	(B)	(C)	(D)	(E)
5	Conditions	Needs of both partners	Local community	All family members	Ceremonies	Advantages
10	+	+	+	+	N	+
15	Satisfy	Meet △	Promise to benefit△	Approve △	Involve	Bring
20	Social ties and financial benefits	Emotional			Formal	Social and financial

Question 11: (A)

Cherry: "despicable, commonplace profligacy" (line 41)

	Essence	(A)	(B)	(C)	(D)	(E)
5	Course	Time	Damage	Other	His family	Artist's imagination
10	—	—	—	—	—	—
15	Profligacy	Wastes	No regret	No respect	Dependent	Lack
20	Commonplace, despicable	Reckless, undignified	Caused by his actions	They deserve	Financial support	

Question 12: (B)

Cherry: "right to claim," (line 56) "to demand" (line58)

	Essence	(A)	(B)	(C)	(D)	(E)
5	Your right to claim	Accusation	Idea	Exaggerations	Earlier claim △	Her right △
10	—	—	—	—	—	+
15	Denying	Denying	Challenging	Correcting △	Contradicting △	Asserting △
20	Answer to that question	Secretly engaged	She must address the question	Implicit in the question	Complete independence	To live without marrying

Question 13: (D)

Cherry: "Our…Sympson?" (line 69)

	Essence	(A)	(B)	(C)	(D)	(E)
5	Keeldar & Sympson	Miss Keeldar	Mr. Sympson	Mr. Sympson	Mr. Sympson	Miss Keeldar
10	—	—	+	—	—	—
15	Different name	Implausible	Serious	Misleading	Baseless	Absurd
20		Outwit	Approval	Genuinely concerned	No real power	Intimidate

Question 14: (A)

Cherry: "scrupulous care" (line 80)

	Essence	(A)	(B)	(C)	(D)	(E)
5	Sympson's warning	Meaning	Blame on him	Tone of his comment	Failure	Behavior
10	–	–	–	–	–	+
15	Playing with	Misunderstand	Turning	Mocking	Lament	Justify
20	Meaning to vex	Deliberately	Scornfully, back	Childishly	Sympathize with her	Previously sensible

Read the question carefully and find the beacon "deflecting." If you return to the text, you will see she seems to be agreeing with Mr. Sympson which seems odd considering our beacon of "deflection" – if you're deflecting something you are pushing it away. Here Miss Keeldar seems to accept and agree with what Mr. Sympson is saying.

This should immediately raise your curiosity – is she being sarcastic, obtuse etc? We now need to examine what she is deflecting – it is the phrase "take care, madam!" So he was originally attacked and now she is responding by counterattacking in her own way. The question is, how? She decides to play with his criticism by turning it around.

Question 15: (D)

Cherry: "unknown tongue," "whether I am comprehended or not" (lines 85-86)

	Essence	(A)	(B)	(C)	(D)	(E)
5	Language	Anything	Wynne's reputation	Speaking manner	Her sentiments	Family's mistakes
10	–	–	–	–	–	–
15	Incomprehensible	Mistrustful	Ignorant △	Obscure △	Incapable of understanding	Unwilling to acknowledge
20		New and unfamiliar	In the community	Inclination		

172 James Hong

Question 16: (B)

Cherry: "Unladylike language!" (line 100) ,"lifted his hands and eyes towards the heavens" (line 101).

	Essence	(A)	(B)	(C)	(D)	(E)
5	Warning	Warning	Prediction	Confession	Plea	Condemnation
10	–	–	–	N	N	–
15	Future	Losses	Future	Relief	Diversion	Lifestyle
20	Gloomy	Financial	Bleak	Own	Unexpected	Conventional

"…to what will she come" is an idiomatic expression of concern for what will happen in the future. If you don't know this expression, there is still the phrase "Unladylike language!" with its accompanying exclamation point to show his implicit warning. Finally, we have the Cherry in which Mr. Sympson physically demonstrates (eyes and hands) that he considers Miss Keeldar to be a desperate failure with poor prospects for the future.

Question 17: (C)

Cherry: "Never to the altar with Sam Wynne" (line 102)

	Essence	(A)	(B)	(C)	(D)	(E)
5	Future	Explanation	Her sense of fair play	Future	Uncertainty △	Family's history
10	N		N	N		N
15	Asking	Request	Appeal △	Inquiry	Express △	Understand
20		Unreasonable			Moral	

Explanation: Miss Keeldar chooses to take Mr. Sympson's words literally and focus on the short term (her potential marriage to Mr. Wynn) in counterattacking Mr. Sympson. This contrasts with Mr. Sympson's intended meaning that she is a desperate case who is acting irrationally. Similar to #14, Miss Keeldar takes what Mr. Sympson says and goads him with his own words.

Question 18: (B)

Explanation: If we look after line 100 according to our Essence Tracking Technique, there isn't any statement by Keeldar regarding love. So now we turn to the General idea of the Passage to see what Keeldar and Sympson's views on love are:

5	Keeldar vs. Love	Sympson vs. Love
10	+	−
15	Important for marriage	Dismissive of it. Money, status is king

This gave us a solid incomplete Essence to use in the Table:

	Essence	(A)	(B)	(C)	(D)	(E)
5	Condition for marriage	Consequence of companionship	Prerequisite	Element △	Accident	Delusion
10	+	N	+	+	+	−
15	Love	Natural	Satisfactory marriage	Desirable	Fortunate	Sentimental △
20		Prolonged	Crucial	Independent woman's daily life	results from marriage	Potentially harmful

Question 19: (E)

Explanation: Here we can again refer to our Table in question #18. This is a general question where we need to put together the aspirations Miss Keeldar has for a marriage (love) and what Mr. Sympson believes is most important (money, status) to get the answer of (D).

	Essence	(A)	(B)	(C)	(D)	(E)
5	Marriage	Marriage	Wynne family	She	Belief	Marriage
10	N	+	+	+	+	N
15	Money and love	Money	Honorable	Mature	Adamant	Poor and undignified
20		Aristocratic				

Literary Devices

Accusation: charging with a fault or offense.

Allegory: The device of using character and/or story elements symbolically to represent an abstraction in addition to the literal meaning. The allegorical meaning usually deals with moral truth or a generalization about human existence.

Anachronism: a chronological inconsistency in some arrangement.

Anticipated objection: a technique a writer or speaker uses in an argumentative text to address and answer objections, even though the audience has not had the opportunity to voice these objections.

Assertion: the act of stating or declaring positively and often forcefully or aggressively

Citation: a reference to a published or unpublished source.

Comparison: the process of representing of one thing or person as similar to or like another

Concession: an admission in an argument that the opposing side has points; to grant, allow or yield to a point.

Contrast: describing the differences between two or more entities

Conundrum:

(1) A riddle whose answer is or involves a pun or unexpected twist.

(2) A logical postulation that evades resolution, an intricate and difficult problem.

Counterargument: an objection to an objection. A counterargument can be used to rebut an objection to a premise, a main contention or a lemma.

Direct quotation: a repetition of someone's exact words.

Disclaimer: a denial of a claim, or any statement intended to specify or delimit the scope of rights and obligations that may be exercised and enforced by parties in a legally recognized relationship.

Dry humor: sarcastic or ironic in nature.

Emotional appeal: pathos. An appeal to the audience's emotions. The pathos of a speech or writing is only ultimately determined by the hearers.

Euphemism: a more agreeable or less offensive substitute for a generally unpleasant word or concept.

Extended analogy: a similarity developed at great length, occurring frequently in or throughout a work.

Figurative language: describing something by comparing it with something else. (e.g. : simile, metaphor, personification…etc)

Historical fact: a piece of information stated in history

Hyperbole: A figure of speech using deliberate exaggeration or overstatement. Often, hyperbole produces irony. The opposite of hyperbole is understatement.

Hypothesis: a proposed explanation for a phenomenon.

Hypothetical scenario: a conjectural scenario

Invocation: the act of petitioning for help or support

Irony: the contrast between what is stated explicitly and what is really meant, or the difference between what appears to be and what is actually true.

Literary allusion: a casual reference in literature to another passage of literature, often without explicit identification.

Metaphor: a literary figure of speech that uses an image, story or tangible thing to represent a less tangible thing or some intangible quality or idea

Overstatement: hyperbole. The use of exaggeration as a rhetorical device or figure of speech.

Paradox: using contradiction in a manner that oddly makes sense on a deeper level.

Parallel structure: the grammatical or rhetorical framing of words, phrases, sentences, or paragraphs to give structural similarity.

Paraphrase: a restatement of the meaning of a text or passage using other words.

Personal anecdote: a short personal narrative account of an amusing, unusual, revealing, or interesting event.

Personification: a figure of speech in which the author describes concepts, animals, or inanimate objects by endowing them with human attributes or emotions.

Qualification: a restriction in meaning or application. Exception.

Rebuttal: a form of evidence that is presented to contradict or nullify other evidence that has been presented by an adverse party.

Repetition: simply the repeating of a word, within a sentence or a poetical line.

Rhetorical questioning: i.e., "What should honest citizens do?" The question often implies an answer, but usually does not provide one explicitly.

Satire: an attack on any stupidity or vice in the form of scathing humor, or a critique of what the author sees as dangerous religious, political, moral, or social standards.

Scholarly analysis: the process of breaking a complex topic into smaller parts in scholastic manner to gain a better understanding of it.

Simile: a figure of speech that directly compares two different things, usually by employing the words "like" or "as."

Speculation: assumption of unusual business risk in hopes of obtaining commensurate gain

Statistical information: information that contains the collection, organization, analysis, and interpretation of data.

Technical jargon: the term covers the language used by people who work in a particular area or who have a common interest.

Understatement: the ironic minimalizing of fact, understatement presents something as less significant than it is. Understatement is the opposite of *hyperbole.*

130 Most Essential SAT Tones

<Positive>

Amused: pleasurably entertained

Dignified: self-respect

Ebullient: enthusiastic, high-spirited

Empathetic: to understand the feeling of another

Evenhanded: fair and just

Exhilarated: enliven, invigorate, stimulate/to make cheerful or merry

Facetious: humorous, amusing

Fervent: enthusiastic, having or showing great warmth or intensity of spirit

Hilarious: extremely funny

Impartial: fair and just

Intrigued: to arouse the curiosity or interest by fascinating qualities, to captivate

Laudatory: expressing praise

Objective: unbiased

Prudent: wise or judicious/sagacious

Reassuring: confidence

Receptive: admitting, willing to receive suggestion

Reverent: deeply respectful

Self-effacing: modest

Unaffected: genuine

Unpretentious: modest

\<Neutral\>

Ambivalence: uncertainty caused by inability to make a choice

Circumspect: watchful and discreet, cautious, prudent

Confidential: indicating confidence or intimacy, imparting private matters

Conversational: colloquial

Emphatic: strongly expressive, expressed with emphasis

Expository: explanatory

Guarded: cautious, careful

Lighthearted: care-free, cheerful

Moralistic: displaying a concern with morality

Nostalgic: a sentimental yearning for the happiness felt in former place, time or situation.

Pensive: wistfully thoughtful/seriously thoughtful often during times of sadness

Pragmatic: pertaining to practical point of view

Profound: having deep insight or understanding

Provocative: acting as a stimulus, inciting, irritating

Reflective: contemplative, thoughtful

Reserved: slow to reveal emotions

Scholarly: learned, academic

Spontaneous: natural, unplanned, resulting from natural impulses

Tempered: made less intense or violent

Tolerant: permissive, incline to tolerate

<Negative>

Adamant: unyielding in attitude, or opinion

Admonishing: reprove or scold in a mild way/ advice, caution

Affected: influenced by external factor

Argumentative: disputatious, contentious

Apathetic: showing little or no emotion

Apprehensive: uneasy or fearful about something that might happen

Baffled: confuse, bewilder

Belligerent: war-lie, hostile, aggressive

Bemused: bewildered or confused

Bewildered: completely puzzled or confused

Callous: insensitive

Capricious: sudden unpredictable changes in attitude or behavior

Caustic: severely critical or sarcastic

Cavalier: haughty, disdainful

Chagrin: feeling annoyed, disappointed, and humiliated

Complacent: pleased without knowing potential danger,

Condemnatory: expressing strong disapproval

Condescending: displaying a patronizingly superior attitude

Confrontational: tending to be aggressive

Contemptuous: expressing disdain

Contrite: showing sincere remorse

Disbelieving: refuse or reject to believe in

Disdainful: scornful,

Disinterested: indifferent, unbiased

Dismayed: dishearten thoroughly, lose confidence

Dismissive: lack of interest, disdainful

Didactic: inclined to teach or lecture

Diffident: lacking confidence in one's own ability

Defiant: boldly resistant or challenging

Derisive: contemptuous, mocking

Despondent: feeling profound hopelessness

Equivocal: dubious, not determined

Exasperation: irritation, extreme annoyance

Flippant: lacking seriousness, disrespectful

Foreboding: a strong inner feeling of a future misfortune, evil

Frivolous: lack of seriousness

Grudging: displaying or reflecting reluctance or unwillingness,

Impassive: without emotion, apathetic

Impetuous: impulsive, sudden action or emotion

Impudent: disrespectful, insulting

Indifferent: without contrast or concern

Indignant: strong displeasure at something considered unjust

Indulgent: overly generous to be lenient with someone

Inflammatory: tending to arouse anger

Inquisitive: excessively curious

Insolent: boldly rude or disrespectful

Irate: angry

Irreverent: disrespectful, flippant

Jaded: exhausted or dissipated

Judgmental: denoting an attitude in which judgment about other people's conduct

Malicious: malevolent, desire to inflict harm on another

Melancholy: sober thoughtful, mournful, depressed

Mocking: to ridicule, to imitate

Morose: gloomily ill-humored

Mundane: common, ordinary

Nonchalant: indifferent or unexcited

Ominous: portending evil or harm

Outrage: strongly offends, insult, or affront the feeling

Partial: biased or prejudiced

Pedantic: ostentatious in one's reading

Peevish: showing annoyance, irritation, or bad mood

Petulant: showing sudden irritation

Pompous: ostentatious display of dignity/pretentious

Pretentious: make oneself more important than one actually is

Quizzical: derisively questioning, ridiculing/odd, queer puzzled

Rebuke: to express sharp stern disapproval of

Reckless: concerned about the consequences of some action

Remorseful: regretting for wrongdoing

Remote: aloof

Resentful: angry at something

Resignation: accepting unwillingly

Resigned: submissive, surrender

Restrained: accepting something undesirable

Revulsion: a strong feeling of repugnance, or dislike

Rueful: feeling sorrow or pity

Sarcastic: harsh or bitter irony

Sardonic: bitter or scornful derision, mocking, cynical

Satirical: use of irony or sarcasm

Self-righteous: confident of oneself, smug

Self-serving: preoccupied with one's own interest disregarding the truth

Severe: harsh, unnecessarily extreme

Smug: excessively self-satisfied

Somber: gloomy, depressing, grave

Studied: not natural, affected

Sullen: showing irritation, ill humor by gloomy silence

Tentative: unsure, uncertain

Unconcern: lack of interest

Whimsical: capricious

Wistful: longing

Wry: bitterly ironic

Flag-Words

Since the best approach to SentCom questions is being simple minded, I have divided all logical relationships into two simple categories: Antonyms and Synonyms. In each sentence, I've boldfaced the Flag-Words and italicized the relevant theme relationships.

For example, in the first sentence below 'but' is our Flag-Word, while '*friendly*' versus '*hostility*' are our contrasting themes.

<Antonym Approach>

1. PIVOTING: reversal

Key Words: **But, however, and yet, while, whereas, on the other hand, in contrast (to), not in the least, without**

- Their mutual joking seemed *friendly,* **but** it masked a long-standing *hostility.*
- Sport can be a *competitive* activity; **however**, it also leads to strong feelings of *camaraderie* among participants.
- *Individual* marketing team members completed their assigned work, **yet** as a *team* they failed to work together.
- **While** a natural talent for taking tests is *helpful* in high school, it *cannot guarantee* success in the real world.
- **Whereas** female students display a natural ability to *manage their time well*, male students often *struggle to complete assigned tasks on time.*
- Summer is a popular season because of its *great weather*; **on the other hand**, this great weather often comes with a lot of *humidity.*
- **In contrast to** the *well written* assignment of David, Steven's assignment had numerous grammatical and spelling *mistakes.*
- He was *relaxed* and **not in the least** *concerned* with his poor performance in class.
- **Without** your *help* with memorizing vocabulary words, Steven's chances of success in the SAT seemed *grim.*

2. **CONESSION**: acknowledge but reverse

Key Words: **Although (though, even though, even if), despite, in spite of, once … now, previously, given**

- **Although** I had a good idea of the *direction* I was going, I still managed to *get lost.*
- **Despite** the *complexity* of this Math problem, the underlying principle is pretty *simple.*
- His well chosen words gave *comfort* to the family, **in spite of** the *sadness* of the occasion.
- **Once** believed to be a *weak* president, Harry Truman is **now** widely regarded as a very *decisive* leader.
- It was **previously** believed David was *lazy*; now however people see he's a *hard worker.*
- His excellent guitar play is all the more remarkable **given** that he was born blind.

3. **NEGATION**: deny and then argue

Key Words: **Not…but…, rather than, far from, free of, indeed, in fact, not so much… as …, actually, seemingly, ironically, paradoxically**

- The importance of the law lies **not** in the way if *forces people to behave*, **but** in its *equalizing effect on society.*
- It's better to *study* **rather than** get a ton of sleep if you want to increase your SAT score.
- Many people believe that an appreciation of the arts, **far from** being a *waste of time, is   important* to instilling creativity.
- **Free of** any *pressure* from that I previously felt, I *can finally tell* you what happened that night.
- Steven's bold speech *didn't* lead people to immediately *follow* him; **instead**, there was a   gradual *increase* in the number of adherents over time.
- I was *arrested* as a suspect, but **in fact**, *didn't even know a crime* had occurred.
- A man's worth lies **not** so **much** in *what he has* as in *what he is.*
- A common idea in Political Science is that power *corrupts* absolutely, when **actually** it's the way this power is used that *leads to the problems.*
- New ideas on food focus on how **seemingly** *insignificant* quantities of fiber can lead to   *substantial* benefits in overall body health.
- **Ironically**, dogs are known to be *peaceful* animals but are responsible for more sheep *deaths* than wolves.

<Synonym Approach>

1. SYMMETRY

<u>Key Words:</u> **just as…so…, much as/like, not only… but also…, and**

- **Just** as humidity is *common* in summer, so *snow is widespread* in the winter.
- I brew a coffee **much like** a *professional barista* does.
- **Much** as a *positive* attitude is important for success, so being optimistic in the face of adversity leads to triumph.
- The new government is faced with **not only** *managing* the disaster **but also** *changing* the way people view governmental services.
- David is *hard working* **and** *intelligent.*

2. APPOSITION

<u>Key Words:</u> **That is, in other words, nothing short of, namely**

- He's extremely *stubborn,* **that** is, *he always wants to get his own way.*
- He *loves talking at length* on topics he's familiar with, **in other words** he's *loquacious.*
- His amazing performance is a **nothing short of** magic.
- There is a distinct *lack of culture in that neighborhood,* **namely** *there are no museums.*

3. PARAPHRASE

<u>Key Tools:</u> **Semi-colon (;), colon(:), hyphen(-)**

- Exercise has the ability to *rejuvenate the body and mind*; just exercising twice a week will leave you *refreshed and mentally in control.*
- Curing them of their superstitions *took years*: even after the local people had been introduced to science they *persisted* in their backward beliefs.
- We saw a *thrilling movie* today – I'm sure it will win an *Oscar.*

4. CAUSE AND EFFECT

Key Words: **Because, since, for, thus, (so) that, so…as to, in that, consequently, therefore, by/through**

- **Because** it's *difficult to measure* how much rain fell yesterday, *we don't know* whether we to expect flooding.
- **Since** she believed him to be *honest*, she *refused* to believe he'd *lied* to her
- The man was *larger than he appeared to be*, **for** he was *diminished* by the perspective, standing in a darkened recess of the chapel.
- The well-trained scientist needs to understand *many fields*; **thus**, a *holistic* curriculum should be followed.
- In his opinion, the neighbors were at *fault*, **so that** to invite them round to visit would just invite more *trouble*.
- The new rules were so *vague* and so devoid of specific advice **as to** make them virtually *meaningless*.
- *Music changes* constantly **in that** each new generation of singer *reinterprets* what it means to make music.
- He'd been in the desert for thirty days; **consequently**, he *greedily drank the water.*
- He *works hard* and **therefore** *earns a lot of money.*
- **By** *removing himself* from bad influences, he successfully *stopped* drinking and smoking.

5. TIME

Key Words: **When, until, since, after, once**

- He *performed well at school* **when** test taking skill was the *most important attribute for a studen*t to have.
- Until you *master* James Hong's techniques, you better not *take the SAT.*
- Ever **since** the internet became available, people's *efficiency* in the workplace has greatly *increased.*
- He knew he was going to *win a prize* **after** his teacher gave him a *wink* during the ceremony.
- **Once** you visit the *Grand Canyon,* you'll know what a truly *spectacular* sight it is.

6.CONDITION

Key Words: **If, given, granted, as long as**

- **If** you bring me *flowers*, I'll write a *love poem* for you.
- **Given** his *remarkable performance* at the theatre, its natural he receives so much *praise*.
- **Granted** that he *did nothing wrong*, I'm sure that he'll be set *free*.
- **As long as** follow the *rules*, you won't get in *trouble*.

7. DEGREE

Key Words: **Stop short of, if not, even**

- He may seem *aggressive* but he **stops short of** actually ever getting *violent*.
- She looks *pretty* **if not** *gorgeous* with the sun shining behind her.
- **Even** the most *heinous* criminal would find that *appalling*.

Glossary

ACET (Answer Choice Evaluation Table): A table used to find differences between Answer Choices (see the solutions to Test 1 for numerous examples of this).

Antonym Approach: used to find the difference between words (usually simplified Answer Choices) by looking at each word's antonym [Refer to Page 168]

Backward Method (Reading):

1) You only read the *italicized* blurb at the top of the passage, ignore the passage and then immediately move to the questions.
2) Skip any General Questions you encounter (General Questions do not have a line reference).
3) Attempt to solve *only* Detail Questions with a line reference by reading the part of the passage the question refers to.
4) Finally, returning to the General Questions, use the general theme you could probably come up with after you've solved the Detail Questions. [Refer to Page 47]

Beacon: A specific piece of information in the Question that directs you to find something in Text [Refer to Page 89]

Bottom Line: a technique used to find the "soul" of an Answer Choice by simplifying it (the Answer Choice) to the greatest extent possible. [Refer to Page 126]

Brad Pitt: outstanding details in the Answer Choice that you can point to and compare with other details (both in other Answer Choices and in the Text). [Refer to Page 122]

Closing: Making a decision on selecting between multiple potentially correct Answer Choices in the Second Round. [Refer to Page 104]

Counterbalancing: the predictable way ETS constructs its Answer Choices. Every incorrect Answer Choice on the SAT will have either its topic (5), evaluation (10), theme (15), or details (20), or even a combination of these not matching the Essence. At the same time there will be correct elements within the 5, 10 and 15 of the Answer Choice. The combination of correct and incorrect elements and how they are assembled is counterbalancing. [Refer to Page 118]

Cherry Picking: a Cherry is something in the Text that helps you find the Essence. In some cases, the Cherry and Essence are exactly the same; in other cases, they're different. [Refer to Page 96]

Detail Questions: either a direct line reference a part of the passage or have a beacon for you to follow [Refer to Page 89]

Direct Questions: obvious information within the Text is being asked for *i.e.* it's easy to see what information ETS wants you to focus on and there is no extended reasoning (unlike Indirect-questions, no stretching is necessary) [Refer to Page 91]

Double Column Question:

 a) double blank questions in SentCom that can't be solved by looking at a single Answer Choice column (left or right)
 b) where there are two or more Answer Choices that seem to have a similar l topic (5), evaluation (10) and theme (15), making it difficult to find an immediate difference between the various Answer Choices. [Refer to Page 112]

Essence: evidence from the Text that allows you to objectively select a correct Answer Choice. [Refer to Page 94]

ETS: Educational Testing Services – the *organization* that developed the SAT

Essence Tracking Technique: a method for finding the Essence within the Text for a beacon-style question where there isn't a line reference. Here we use the prior and subsequent questions' line references to target the Essence. [Refer to Page 90]

First Round: the time during which you're *only* sorting questions into either the O or X-question categories within a minimum amount of time. [Refer to Page 34]

Forward Reading: the way you've solved reading comprehension questions your whole life –by reading the text and then answering the questions. [Refer to Page 48]

General Questions: don't reference any specific location in the paragraph/passage and don't have a beacon. [Refer to Page 89]

Half-Known: An element within the Text (this could be a word, sentence of paragraph) where objective meaning isn't 100% clear. [Refer to Page 66]

Hierarchy of Importance: a principle that pieces of information in the Table have different levels of importance when we're trying to find an incomplete Essence [Refer to Page 133]

Indirect Questions: reference specific parts of the text but the link between the question and the text is still a bit hazy. These questions often contain wording such as "imply", "suggest", "assumes", "infer" etc. [Refer to Page 91]

Known: An element within the Text (this could be a word, sentence of paragraph) where objective meaning is 100% clear. [Refer to Page 100]

Macro Management: an overarching technique that is mainly concerned with time management [Refer to Page 20]

Mr. Simple: A testing personality that's good at summarizing and seeing the big picture [Refer to Page 28]

Micro Management: a collection of techniques we use to simplify and analyze questions, answer choices and the text and ultimately find the correct answer [Refer to Page 84]

Mr. Complex: A testing personality that's very detail oriented and can be a liability in the First Round [Refer to Page 27]

Moneyball Approach: a system of increasing your overall odds of doing well in the SAT by marginally raising the chances you'll get questions right and marginally reducing the chances that you'll get answer wrong. [Refer to Page 11]

Objective Critical Reading: reaching conclusions about an author's intentions by finding stated evidence within the Text [Refer to Page 77]

Optimal Test Taker (OTT): an excellent Macro Manager. This kind of test taker knows what types of questions to attack and when to do it. He doesn't waste time on questions that are not appropriate for his base critical reading level and excels at simplifying complex concepts and ideas [Refer to Page 28]

O-question: you read the question, read the answer choices and easily find the answer you're looking for (locating the answer should be virtually instantaneous) [Refer to Page 34]

PBR: Passage Based Reading [Refer to Page 22]

Second Round: The time during which you're no longer sorting questions but rather attacking them using techniques outlines in Micro Management [Refer to Page 41]

SentCom: Sentence Completion [Refer to Page 22]

Single Column Question:

    a) a single blank question in SentCom;

    b) a double blank question in Sentcom that we can solve by looking at only one Answer Choice column (either left or right);

    c) a question where the Answer Choices are fundamentally different based on the topic (5), evaluation (10), and theme (15) of each Answer Choice.[Refer to Page 109]

Table Buddy: a tool used to dissect elements (words, sentences, paragraphs, passages) for analysis [Refer to Page 50]

Theme Matching: ability to "see" hidden synonyms within parts of the Text (words, sentences, paragraphs, and passages) and eventually make connections with the Answer Choices [Refer to Page 55]

Top-Down (TD): a method for finding an incomplete Essence. Top-Down gets its name from the way we use information in the Table to try find an incomplete Essence – we process information from the top of the Table and move down. [Refer to Page 99]

Triangle Question: To be able to mark a question as Δ-questions you must either:

    a) know the answer but find two answer choices that seem to fit (one answer choice should seem like a slightly better fit) or;

    b) *don't* know the answer but can eliminate three obviously incorrect answer choices, leaving you with two answer choices (one answer choice should seem like a slightly better fit). [Refer to Page 45]

What Questions: focus on parts of the Text where something isn't completely clear. There is a piece of the puzzle missing, and it's your job to look at the Text and find the missing puzzle piece [Refer to Page 91]

Why Questions: look at how the passage or paragraph was constructed and explain why the author chose to, for example, use a quotation mark, insert an unusual term, or write the passage. [Refer to Page 92]

X-question: when you attempt this type of question you either chose avoid it because you didn't have a strong Essence or, with a strong Essence, you tried to solve the question but couldn't because there wasn't an immediate, clear correct answer (this is all in the First Round). You would omit this kind of question. [Refer to Page 34]

(5) **Topic**: the subject of a word, sentence, paragraph or passage and the easiest piece of information to find [Refer to Page 52]

(10) **Evaluation**: a subjective measure of the positive (+) or negative (-) connotations that are associated with a word, sentence, paragraph or passage. [Refer to Page 52]

(15) **Theme**: provides more information about the Topic - a kind of loose summary of whatever you're examining [Refer to Page 52]

(20) **Details**: extra information that surround the topic and theme [Refer to Page 52]

5/4/6/9 Section: a common Section construction consisting of 5 SentCom questions, 2 Short Passages with 4 accompanying questions, 1 Mid-length Passage with 6 accompanying questions and a Long Passage with 9 accompanying questions [Refer to Page 47]

8/4/12 Section: a common Section construction consisting of 8 SentCom questions, 2 Short Passages with 4 accompanying questions and a Long Passage with 12 accompanying questions [Refer to Page 47]

6/13 Section: a common Section construction consisting of 6 SentCom questions and a Long passage with 13 accompanying questions. [Refer to Page 47]